Over a Cup of Coffee

Musings by V.N. Kakar

Publishers
Pustak Mahal®, Delhi

J-3/16 , Daryaganj, New Delhi-110002
☎ 23276539, 23272783, 23272784 • *Fax:* 011-23260518
E-mail: info@pustakmahal.com • *Website:* www.pustakmahal.com

Branch Offices
Bangalore: ☎ 22234025
E-mail: pmblr@sancharnet.in • pustak@sancharnet.in
Mumbai: ☎ 22010941
E-mail: rapidex@bom5.vsnl.net.in
Patna: ☎ 3094193 • *Telefax:* 0612-2302719
E-mail: rapidexptn@rediffmail.com
Hyderabad: *Telefax:* 040-24737290
E-mail: pustakmahalhyd@yahoo.co.in

Edition : October 2005

ISBN 81-223-0916-X

Printed at : Param Offsetters, Okhla, New Delhi-110020

Contents

PREFACE

From shaking hands with M.A. Jinnah in Peshawar and saying good-buy to Lord Mountbatten in Shimla, rubbing shoulders with the high and mighty in Delhi and getting lost amongst the common people of India, to watching the little kids helping my wife with bags of fruits in hand to negotiate the thirty-six steps to our nest in the Tara Apartments – every situation in which I was involved or to which I have been a witness, has left some little trail behind it.

Emerging from this trail are countless middles, the Lord has enabled me to scribble. Some have a message to throw up. Some may make you pause and think. And some may just enable you to take life as it is and smile your way through it.

I am grateful to the many newspapers and magazines that have been kind enough to publish my middles and musings. These include *The Times of India*, *The Hindustan Times*, *The Indian Express*, *The Statesman*, *The Tribune*, *The Pioneer*, *The late Evening News*, *The Patriot*, *Illustrated Weekly of India*, *Eve's Weekly* and Krishna Kripalini's *Vigil*. I am equally grateful to many of my readers who keep on sending warm letters to me.

The number of my published middles and musings would now be 3,000 approximately. However, for this little book, I have selected about 120 middles.

—V.N. Kakar

DEDICATION

Dedicated to my parents,
my wife, Shakuntala, our children,
Renu and Harsh,
Prem and Rita,
Rita and Ashok.

Anything wrong happening anywhere in the world, the poor old bus in Delhi has to pay the price for it, partly at least.

Bent by age, crushed by heavy responsibilities, wounded in battles several times but mentioned in despatches not even once, it goes on performing its patriotic duty of carrying people from one place to another in a manner worthy of great heroes.

It goes off the roads only when it is compelled to do so – by a *bandh* or curfew or some serious self-inflicted wound. If it had been in America or Japan, it would have by now been dumped into the sea or crushed into powder.

In India, off and on it goes to its workshop – home for old people (they call them senior citizens now), where it is renovated, rejuvenated and given a further lease of life. Once back on the road, it faces the same onslaughts – physical, psychological and biological. Be it Mandal or Ayodhya, Iraq or Israel, or students' boredom with their studies, the bus must be stoned. And it must not grumble.

Think of the great causes it serves, apart from shortening distances for people who travel by it. It brings them together, be they from the North or the South, East or West. It promotes national integration like nothing else does. It absorbs their indiscipline, their impatience, their anger, their antics. And in the process, it strengthens their faith in their own destiny and confidence in their ability to make it. Howsoever crowded the bus may be, they know that they can enter it. And they do enter. If they fail to do so, they stand on the foot-boards or hang by the railings at the rear-end.

My admiration is particularly great for that remarkable piece of ingenuity called the mini-bus. In appearance it is like a small hearse car but in performance it is like the large-hearted throw-away cigarette lighter which, unlike in other countries, we in India don't like to throw away as soon as the gas in it has given us its last flame. We go on using it by getting it refilled with cooking gas or whatever it is. The boys who sell imported goods in the tire bazaars do it gladly at Rs 2 per piece.

I must confess that I do not have much experience of transport by bus, particularly by mini-bus, in Delhi. But heeding to all these 'save petrol' calls, I had to take a mini-bus on Jan. 31, 1991, for going from Tara Apartments to Kasturba Gandhi Marg. Ominously, it bore the No. 13. As I approached it, I found it full to the brim. But the conductor encouraged me to walk in. He also took in many more and asked us all to move ahead to make way for others.

There was no such thing as 'ahead'. Many passengers were standing in the narrow lane between the two rows of seats, all occupied. Moving ahead meant that we should sit on others' shoulders. Still, at every stop the conductor took more passengers and repeated his 'move ahead' slogan. The bus was intended for no more than 20 persons. Its capacity enlarged at every stop it touched. By the time it reached Khan Market, it had, I suspect, nearly 70. Throughout it moved fast and took sharp turns. At several points people fell one over another.

When the Kasturba Gandhi stop came, it became difficult for me to get out. The conductor was kind enough to ask other standing passengers to make way for me, which they did. As he himself also came out to take more passengers, I asked him, "is it the peak hour?"

"*Nahin, Janab*," he chuckled, "it is the *abadi* hour. In our country all time is *abadi* time. If the people go on increasing like this, we shall soon have to build another storey on our poor little bus."

■■

Bath in London

On a brief visit to London from the Sussex University in Brighton, where I was a study fellow in the mid-seventies, I happened to stay at the residence of a friend's relative. I had not known him earlier, but, being on a meagre allowance, I took advantage of his generous offer to spend the night with him rather than in a hotel.

He had a two-bed-room flat not far away from South Hall where most Indians and Pakistanis live. His wife was working in a post office and his two teen-aged daughters were studying in a school. He himself was a salesman in some concern.

The bed-rooms were on the first floor and the drawing room and the kitchen on the ground.

There was a small improvised dining room below the staircase. It was a modest house belonging to a modest man who had a large heart.

Adjoining the drawing room, in which I spent the night on a sofa-cum-bed, was a bathroom. In the morning when I wanted to use it, I discovered that it had a wall-to-wall carpet. The gentleman's wife had placed for me a new towel on the towel-stand and a new cake of soap in the soapbox. Above the bath-tub, which was made of white cement or marble, there were two taps, one for hot water and the other for cold. But the tub itself was surrounded by the carpet. So was the space around the WC and below the wash-basin.

How to take your bath in a bath-tub without allowing the water to sprinkle outside it? I did not know that art and skipped my bath. While shaving, I took special care to ensure that nothing fell outside the wash-basin. Some foam from the brush did fall on the carpet. I wiped it off with the towel.

In London, as elsewhere in Europe, people are used to 'dry-cleaning'. In France, they have community bathrooms, to use which one has to pay a tidy sum. My host, as he told me later, did have a proper bathroom; I mean one without a carpet. But that was on the first floor, between the two bed-rooms, and despite his pleas, I did not think it proper to use it.

"No bathrooms in my house, only glamour rooms," says the charming girl in the TV advertisement. She is promoting some sanitaryware – wash-basins, tubs, cisterns and things like that, all installed inside a bathroom. The focus is on the shapes and shades and curves and contours of the stuff as well as on the girl, first shown in a gown and then fully dressed. I suppose in between her two appearances, she must have taken her bath.

Where – if she does not have a bathroom in her house? Or, if the bathroom has a wall-to-wall carpet, as was my experience that night in London?

Well, I don't know the answer to the question. Maybe we are coming close to that point in time when the good old saying 'inner cleanliness comes first' becomes as good a joke as was the recent Earth Summit in Rio de Janerio.

■■

"There are two kinds of pumpkins" said my wife, "one is long and green, it's called *kaddu*. The other is round and yellow. It is called *petha*. In Delhi, people sometimes refer to both as *kaddu*. Don't get confused. Bring *petha* and not *kaddu*. The *sabziwali* outside the Yamuna Apartments knows. Tell her that Tara Apartments-*wali mataji* has sent you. She will understand."

I went straight to the *sabziwali* outside the Yamuna Apartments. I had to. My wife was down with pain and the doctor had advised her not to climb even staircases. Buying vegetables in normal times is exclusively her responsibility. She doesn't want me even to accompany her while discharging this responsibility.

She thinks that if I do, people always quote high rates. I have never been able to understand the logic behind her argument. In any case, I am not bothered. It suits all husbands not to try to understand many things their wives do or say. And that's God's truth.

The *sabziwali* outside the Yamuna Apartments was kind enough to enquire about *mataji*'s health and understood what she required. Still, in order not to risk anything, I asked a young South Indian lady also buying vegetables whether the round pumpkin the *sabziwali* had given was the same that my wife had asked me to bring. She looked at me, smiled and said it was the same, adding helpfully that the Punjabis called it *petha* also.

She also explained to me that *petha* had the same colour inside as outside, while *kaddu* was white inside and green on the outside. I enquired the rate from the *sabziwali*. She said magnanimously, "for others, it is 10 rupees a kilo, for you, it is eight rupees. How much shall I weigh out for you?"

The question floored me completely. For while my wife had explained to me the difference between *kaddu* and *petha*, she had forgotten to mention the quantity I should buy. I looked towards the young South Indian lady again, almost imploringly, and requested her to tell me how much I should purchase. "That," she retorted smilingly, "depends on how much you would like to eat."

"We are just two," I said, "and we are not heavy eaters."

"In that case" said the lady, bursting into a laugh, "one kilo should suffice."

I bought a kilo of the darned thing and lugged it home. My wife was happy that I had passed the test. The credit for this, of course, goes to the unknown but gentle South Indian lady. For if she happens to read this piece, may I say, "Thank you, kindly Madame".

■■

We have a lovely dark brown Labrador bitch. Just about a year old, it is well behaved, affectionate and responsible. Like all Labradors, it finds it difficult to stand the heat of Delhi. So, during summer, it sleeps in the upper floor bedroom of my son Prem and daughter-in-law Rita just below their airconditioner.

As morning comes, the newspaper boy throws up our papers, duly rolled and held securely with the aid of a rubber band, in the gallery which we share with an illustrious neighbour. That gentleman subscribes to one newspaper. We get three. Hence our bundle is bulkier than his. Anyone with eyes open can detect that without wasting any time.

The moment our bundle hits our door, Brandy rushes out, picks it up and takes it straight to Rita and Prem's bedroom. Brandy knows what bundle is for what flat. It makes no mistake in picking the one intended for us.

Call it curiosity, senility or whatever else, lately it has invaded our neighbour. Sometimes he steals a march over Brandy, picks up our bundle, opens it, runs through the headlines in the papers to which he himself does not subscribe, rolls all of them back in position, though clumsily, and drops them quietly at our door.

Sometimes when Brandy takes longer to come down or when he finds something gripping in the papers which he himself does not get, he takes the whole lot inside his house.

When Brandy comes out and finds our bundle missing, it sniffs around to detect where it has gone. And then it rushes back to see if Sushma, our cook, has not already taken it there.

No, that is not the case. Brandy comes back, sniffs around again, knocks at the neighbour's door with its front paws and out comes the bundle in a huddle through the window. Brandy stares at the gentleman's flat angrily, picks up our bundle and takes it straight to the bedroom.

Diamonds may be for ever, but not wrong things. The Lord won't allow that. One fine morning, our call-bell, fixed at the door-frame but connected to the kitchen, started ringing non-stop. It sounded like a siren announcing another Indo-Pakistan war. Thinking that Sushma was perhaps in the bathroom, my son came down, opened the door and found our neighbour standing there with a mighty grievance on his lips. "What is it, Uncle?" the boy, a doctor, asked him, thinking perhaps that an acute pain had suddenly gripped the man's head or stomach. "It looks," said he, "that your dog has taken away my paper as well." The boy explained to him that to the best of his knowledge, Brandy was not prone to do that kind of thing. As a rule, it picked up its own papers only and brought them straight to him.

Brandy was summoned. Whenever it does some mischief, it hides itself under the dining table. It came out, looked at the man, measured him from head to foot, went up, brought his solitary paper from wherever it had kept it and threw it at him with utmost contempt. The gentleman said nothing to it. What could he say?

Months have elapsed since that episode. Our papers no longer disappear from where the newspaper boy throws them up.

■■

Somewhere in its lost property pits the Government of India might still be resting a bulky file on *paan masala*. When Ashok Kumar and Shammi Kapoor joined hands to promote its sale, Nirman Bhavan – the HQ of the Ministry of Health and Family Welfare (both subjects incidental) – went on fire.

Shammi Kapoor comes to the house of Ashok Kumar along with his wife. Ashok Kumar's daughter is to be married to Shammi Kapoor's son. The Kumars think that the Kapoors had come with a fresh demand for dowry. *Hamein kuchh nahin chahiye* (we don't need anything), Shammi assures Ashok Kumar, "all that we want is that you should greet the *barat* with *paan masala*."

Life returns to Ashok Kumar, as well as to his wife. Ashok Kumar takes a tin of *paan masala* from his pocket, laughs heartily, and tells Shammi, "I never knew that, like me, you, too, are terribly sold on *paan masala*."

That little ad. on TV caused a big jump in the sale of *paan masala*. And this was causing concern all round. For it was known that chewing *paan masala* was as injurious to health as was cigarette-smoking. Numerous public-spirited organisations had come out with studies making that point. And there was a widespread demand that *paan masala* should be banned.

What should be banned? And what should not be? What should be promoted? And what should not be? In the GOI, there are numerous committees that take care of all such matters. Some are statutory, some non-statutory; some high-power, some with no power; some standing; some sitting; and some (possibly many) sleeping. In the Health Ministry, they have a technical committee with the Director-General, Health Services, as Chairman, and all the luminaries under him as well as in the ICMR (Indian Council of Medical Research) as distinguished members.

That committee, (generally sleeping, I presume), met a number of times and took the view that notwithstanding opposition from the *paan masala* fraternity, the darned thing should be banned forthwith.

But, then, as good old Shakespeare says in *Hamlet*, "there are more things in heavens and on earth, Oh Horatio, than are dreamt of in your philosophy." The committee failed to take cognizance of two formidable factors. One, a bloke called marketing executive (ME) who had come from the marketing field and was responsible for marketing health, whatever that means. And two, a gentleman called Mantriji, who was on the best of terms with the ME. Both of them were known to be great believers in making hay while the sun shines.

So *paan masala* was never banned. Its sale continues to go up. What happened to the file on it? That is more than I can tell. All that I can say is that those were the days when, as now, India was having too much of democracy and many people in a number of ministries did not know who their latest minister was.

■■

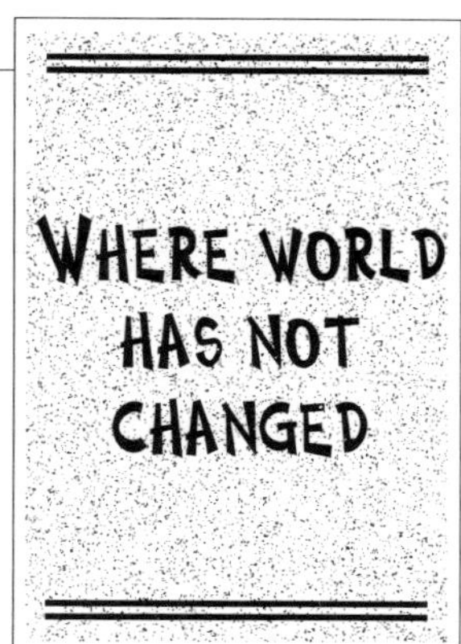

In 1939-40, I was a student for a brief period in the S.A. Jain College in Ambala City. We were living in the cantonment, some five miles away, where my father was posted. I used to go to my college by train. There were about 20 other students living in the cantonment who did the same. The only other mode of transport was the tonga. That took a long time. Besides, there were some hillocks between the Ambala Cantonment and the city. That was supposed to be risky.

In those days, the trains had four classes – I, II, Inter and III. There was no AC class. We used to travel third and the cost of the monthly ticket was Rs 2. On return journey, the train coming from the Rajpura side was often late. We would discover this only after reaching the city station from our college. It was difficult to pass the time at the railway station. How much mischief could one make?

The station master, knowing that boys would be boys, used to lock up the Second Class waiting-room. He would not allow us to enter it since we were Third Class passengers. One day, one of us purchased a Second Class ticket from Ambala city to the cantonment. It cost four annas. On its strength, the student forced the station master to open the Second Class waiting-room. He walked into it triumphantly. The rest of us followed him.

The next day, another student purchased the Second Class ticket. But while he walked into the Second Class waiting-room without any difficulty, the rest of us were prevented from doing so. There was a row between us and the station staff. It could not last for ever. Eventually, the station master, despite the fact that he had at his backing the full might of the British Empire, had to yield. Turn by turn, one of us would buy the Second Class ticket and on its strength, the rest of us would spend the waiting period in the Second Class waiting-room. That was great fun.

In the last week of August 1993, I was going from the Central Secretariat to the Tara Apartments in a Blue-Line bus. Somewhere *en route* about a dozen little school girls in their uniform got in. The bus was already jampacked. The girls managed to squeeze in.

"Take the ticket at least, Guddi," shouted the conductor, smiling at one of them. "Today is the turn of Munni," replied the girl. Munni flung her ticket before the conductor's eyes.

"What about the rest of you?" the man asked the other girls. "Everyday you put the same question to us," said some of them almost in chorus, "and everyday we give you the same reply. One has bought; that is enough. That suffices for others too!"

■■

Sitting in what is considered to be a city of philistines, it is difficult to gauge the intensity of the heat that has been generated in Calcutta by Khushwant Singh's assessment of Rabindranath Tagore's literary talent.

But one can well imagine *bhadraloks* and *bhadramahilas* departing from their cultivated snobbery to disparage the sardar of Sujan Singh Park. In between sips from her glass of gin and tonic at the Tolly, Mrs Mukherjee wrinkles her nose and tells Mrs Ghosh, "But it is only to be expected from him... after all, the only culture he knows about is agriculture." Mrs Ghosh, in between appreciating Mrs Mukherjee's exquisite Tangail, nods her head vigorously as Mr. Chatterjee, after berating the bearer for serving him warm beer, adds scornfully, "What does he know of *Rabindrasanskriti*?"

We could replicate the scene and change the characters. The thrust of the conversation would be much the same: Banerjee*babu*, lower division clerk at Calcutta Municipal Corporation, will spend the entire day telling his colleagues how "injustice has once again been done to Calcutta and Bengali sentiments trampled upon"; at a poky little "cafe" in Gariahat, a group of young men and women will spend the evening debating the relevance of Tagore over shared cups of tea and *kabiraji* cutlet; Saturday afternoons at College Street Coffee House will be spent discussing why Khushwant Singh should be ignored.

Of course, he should be ignored, especially when he seeks to seize the highground of literary criticism and indulges in defamation of the dead and the living. Surely a person who promotes a plagiarist as a writer of outstanding quality is no judge of true literary merit.

But the fact remains that his comments on Tagore have not been ignored. On the contrary, they have been taken seriously enough to trigger demonstrations and furious letters to the editors of Calcutta's English and vernacular newspapers. One commentator has found it fit to write an entire article on why Khushwant Singh cannot be punished for defamation because of loopholes in the law.

There is something ironical about the Bengalis' attachment to Tagore. While the poet has been appropriated as a symbol of Bengal's perceived cultural superiority and made into a god, not many Bengalis care to study his works.

■■

"What kind of hair-cut will you have? English, French or plain Indian?" Baghi Jaan asked me. I did not know what was what and so requested Baghi Jaan to enlighten me on the varieties he had mentioned. "English," said he, "means that there will be a parting; left or right, you decide. And French means no parting at all." "What about Indian?" I asked. "Football ground," he replied, "barren land, total baldness."

Baghi Jaan, Kale Khan, brothers or cousins, I don't know, had opened a salon in Peshawar. It bore the grand name of Aalishan Hair Dressing Salon. The only salon I had known till then, early forties, was the one in Anarkali in Lahore called Victoria. There, they used to charge one rupee for hair-cut and shampoo. I had a girlfriend living in Mahabir Gali No. 2, Nisbet Road. Before going to meet her, against the wishes of her great father, I used to go through my upgrading at Victoria.

Baghi Jaan, Kale Khan were no match for Victoria. Theirs was the first salon in Peshawar city. "Why don't you make it," I said to Baghi Jaan, "as it is now, clipping all that is surplus, I mean all that has outgrown?" He picked up his razor, rubbed it on his leather strap to make it sharper and took it menacingly towards my head. "What the hell are you going to do?" naturally I asked him. "Keep quiet," said he ominously, "this is only for your side-burns. But if you go on chirping while I am on my job, I can't say where my razor may land. If it lands on your throat, God alone may take care of you."

I had to keep quiet and let Baghi Jaan play havoc with my head according to his own whims. As he was engaged in his marvellous job, I could not help reading a glass-framed Urdu verse atop the mirror confronting me. It said, "*Husnwale, husn ka anjam dekh; doobte suraj ko waqt-e-shaam dekh* (Oh you beautiful one, look at the end of your beauty; look at the fate of the sun at the time of sunset)."

Naturally, I was amazed. That was not the kind of thing that went well at a hair-dressing salon. There, they make you look more beautiful day by day. The verse in the glass-frame proclaimed something altogether different.

"Do you know what it means?" I asked Baghi Jaan. "*Kala akshar, bhains barabar* (to me, all script is just like buffalo)" – was his philosophical reply. "In the Kissa Kahani bazar," he added, "the man was selling everything for two and a half annas. I liked the frame and bought it from him." When I explained to him the meaning of the verse, he was shocked. "*Khanzir ki aulad* (pig's son)," said he, "he has cheated me. I will have it out on him."

God knows what Baghi Jaan did thereafter. All that I know is that he removed that framed Urdu verse quickly from atop the mirror.

Long years have gone by. Suddenly that salon of Baghi Jaan, Kale Khan has returned to me. It has obviously returned because I have been reading too much about what Musharraf and company have been doing in Pakistan and Afghanistan – creating the monster called Taliban, arming it, instigating it, giving it all manner of help and now assisting America in destroying it.

■■

On the day of his marriage, a bridegroom in Peshawar had to pass through seven interesting stages before getting on to his bride's place. One, he had to take bath in cold or lukewarm water, a few drops of Gangajal mixed in it. Two, he had to put on a freshly-made boski (expensive silk) salwar and kameez Pathan suit.

Three, and that was something unique to Peshawar, he had to allow young girls and kids, related, of course, to tear off that suit here and there. No, nobody would go to the extent of stripping him naked. They would just come, tease him and participate in the tearing ritual, taking care that the bits they tore did not expose him absolutely.

Four, he would then allow himself to be turned into a perfect buffoon. That meant new Western suit in the case of sarkari mulazims and another made-to-order Pathan suit in the case of those in business. The dominant thing in both situations was the golden-threaded kulah and highly-expensive mushaddi lungi atop his head. Hanging by that headgear and covering his face completely would be dense but not heavy rows of jasmine flowers held together by a solitary string. He could see everybody from that fascinating curtain.

Those interested could see him likewise.

Five, he would be made to mount a white horse or mare. His mother and father and elder sisters and bhabhis would come forward and move their right hand full of currency notes round his headgear. That was known as sirwarna. The money thus taken round was then passed on to the master of the band that had to accompany the marriage procession.

Six, the bloke was put on auction. It was called tambol. That meant that anyone wishing to give any money to his parents on that auspicious occasion was welcome to do that. One man would count the money thus given and then announce "Rs 500 as tambol from Rai Bahadur Hukam Chand Chopra, the bridegroom's uncle." The name of the giver and the money given had to be repeated. To keep the record for future use, another man would jot that down in a notebook.

Seven, the horse or mare would then start moving, with the band playing loudly and relatives and friends dancing merrily. The bridegroom's father would come forward, take fistfuls of coins from a coloured, silken bag, move those coins round the boy's head, symbolically and throw them backward. Little boys and girls took special pleasure in collecting those coins.

I never had the privilege of becoming a bridegroom in Peshawar. Before my time could come, I was kicked out of that town in 1947. But the drama of those lovely rituals comes to my mind as I see the bridegrooms of our democracy, our worthy MPs, getting ready to march into the new Parliament with their breasts swollen legitimately. And I hear myself whispering to myself: "Good ladies and gentlemen, now that we have elected you, for God's sake, start grappling with the problems that pinch you not but pinch the rest of us all."

■■

Fed up with life, a man in some city in the US decides to commit suicide. He goes to the river to drown himself in it. Evening has set in. Still there are people on the bank, indulging in frolics. He does not want that anyone should see him and try to prevent him from doing what he is bent upon. Nothing fails like failure in suicide.

He waits for the people to depart. They are in no hurry. He takes a cab and goes to the bridge. There he leaves the cab and walks up to the middle. He stops there and surveys the scene around to make sure that nobody is watching him. Then he lifts his arms, bends himself on the bridge-railing, raises his feet and falls down.

A photographer is watching him. The man has not seen him. But the photographer has sensed what he is up to. He focuses his camera on him and takes his snaps in the sequence in which the man performs his act successfully.

One of these snaps, showing the man falling into the river, turns out to be the best photograph of the year in the U.S. It is carried by several magazines and gets numerous awards. The photographer becomes a millionaire.

A controversy starts simultaneously. Was it not the moral duty of the photographer to prevent the man from committing suicide when he knew that he was going to do it? Was it proper on his part to allow his personal, professional interest to stifle the voice of his conscience? Did he have a conscience at all? Or did he have two consciences? One as a photographer and one as a human being?

There was a debate on the subject in several magazines. Moralists took the view that instead of being awarded prizes, the photographer should have been hauled up by the police and put behind bars. Some of those belonging to his fraternity said, on the other hand, that the job of a photographer was to capture an event and not to prevent it.

I do not remember when exactly the episode took place. Perhaps it was in the early fifties. Those were the days when I used to subscribe to so many magazines. Several of them are dead. To others, I hardly have any access now. But roaming about early morning in the Jahanpanah City Forest on the outskirts of Delhi, talking to trees, whispering to the wind, chirping with the birds, I often recede into the past which has a remarkable quality of throwing up its treasures when it thinks that it is necessary for man to have a look at them again.

Mother Nature reigns supreme in this forest. She seems to be telling me all the time —

One impulse from a vernal wood

May teach you more of man,

Of moral evil and of good,

Than all the sages can.

I find countless people, young and old, men and women, taking vigour from her. Some walk briskly, some run, some jog, some take yogic exercises. They are all full of life. And the zeal to live longer.

In this beautiful environment, that episode about the photographer and the man who committed suicide has started floating before my eyes. The past has thought it necessary to throw itself up. I do not know for certain why. Perhaps it is because I have been reading too much about conscience and all that in relation to a certain Supreme Court Judge and the impeachment debate on him in Parliament. Or the submergence of the commodity called conscience in election time.

■■

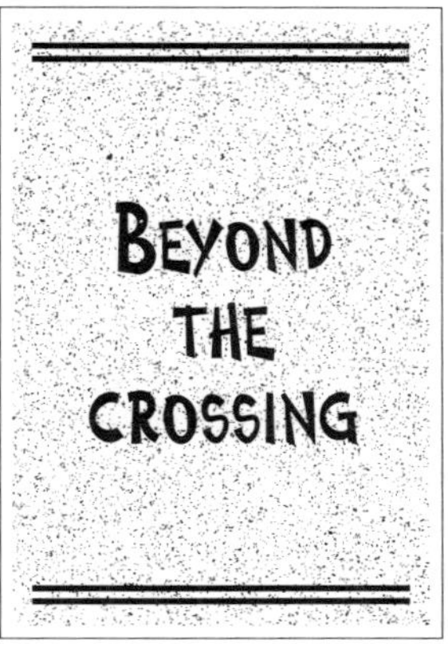

BEYOND THE CROSSING

It was one of the hottest days in May. Evening had set in and night was about to swallow it. That is the time when people, boxed up in their flats, move on to the roads to breathe the coolness which the sunset normally brings. But the heat that day was as oppressive in the open as behind closed doors. I did not find many people on the road.

An old man, his profile familiar, was walking ahead of me near the Don Bosco School in Alaknanda. Another old man, his profile equally familiar, came from the opposite direction of Greater Kailash-II. The two exchanged greetings and then the GK man took a turn and they started walking together in the some direction.

"Lalaji, you have crossed all limits," said the GK man, "So much fire is not bursting from the sky that taking off your shirt, you should be roaming about in the streets of Delhi in a mere *banyaan*. Children will laugh at you."

"Children laugh at me any way", said the Don Bosco man, "wearing or not wearing a shirt is immaterial. But tell me one thing. What is the difference between my *banyaan* and their T-Shirt? My *banyaan* has at least the colour of *sharifan* (gentleman). It is white. The T-shirts they wear have more colours than even the Lord has invented. Some are as red as if these have just come from the oven. Some are green like grass in *barsat* and some are black like *charcoal*.

"And what *anapshanap* (nonsense) is not written on them? I love you. Kiss me. Keep away. Have you ever seen a turban on a boy's head?"

"Yes," said the GK man, "they wear them when their fathers die." Both laughed heartily. "But then", the GK man went on, "what you are saying about T-shirts is correct. Times have changed. In our days, fashion used to start in London and then come to India. Now it starts in Connaught Place and then goes to *villayat* via Karol Bagh. That, however, does not mean that you should do your *muttergashti* (wandering) in a mere *banyaan*."

The situation was amusing. Two persons, apparently in the same circumstances, passing a few moments of their lives together, giving some comfort to each other – talking as I was, almost at the same pace at which they were walking, I could not help listening to their "sweet nothings".

As their outing ended, the GK man said to the Don Bosco man a bit loudly, "Better move on to the other side of the road. But don't cross it here. Cross it where they have those large white lines. They say that if you are over-run by a car on a zebra crossing, your children will get double compensation."

■■

The Nawab of Hoti, like quite a few other rajas and maharajas of the pre-1947 age, was a British creation. Hoti was a part of Mardan district of NWFP. The nawab who, I suspect, had much in common with Osama bin Laden, had made his mark as a dare-devil knight of the British Empire. He could subdue the Pathans like Hari Singh Nalwa had done it under Maharaja Ranjit Singh. The British wanted to reward him appropriately. More importantly, they wanted to keep him on their side eternally. So they carved Hoti out of Mardan, converted it into a princedom and made the nawab its ruler. Further, they bestowed on him the title of hony. captain.

God knows what great strategic significance Hoti had in those days. Of course, NWFP as a whole, situated as it was on this side of Afghanistan, was strategically highly important. There was always the danger that tribal chieftains with their hordes from across the border might any day descend on it and spread over the rest of India. It had happened numerous times earlier. The Hindukush mountains had scattered here and there crushed bones of old warriors. I saw those crushed bones a number of times while taking strolls on the Khyber Pass in the company of my British teachers and other students of the Islamia College, Peshawar, now elevated as a university.

Whatever it was, the British decided to get Hoti back from the nawab. They offered him huge amounts of bribe and a permanent pension. That kind of thing was not unknown in those days. The lovely hill station of Murree, some 50 miles upwards of Rawalpindi, was purchased by them from its erstwhile owner for two twenties (20×2 – Rs. 40). That was quite a big sum in those days. The British wanted Murree very much. Rawalpindi was the HQ of

Northern Command. It was O.K. in winter. But for summer, like Shimla, the British wanted some cool place. Murree was the obvious choice.

Hoti was not a hill station like Murree or Shimla. Yet the British wanted it back. But the nawab, a self-respecting Pathan feudal lord as he was, refused to oblige them and part with his princedom. The British then played their trump card.

The nawab had a young son. The British made him an hony. colonel. Mighty happy and proud, the boy, donning the crown and two stars of a full-fledged colonel, walked into his dad's room. The dad did not recognise him instantaneously since he had never seen him in uniform. He got up from his seat and mistaking him for a big British officer, saluted him in the right royal manner. The boy saluted back. But as he got close to him and as the Nawab of Hoti discovered who he was, he gave him a resounding slap on the face, the sound of which almost brought the Hindukush mountains down on the two of them.

I can't say what happened thereafter. But as I recall that incident, it occurs to me that there is a lesson in it for all of us, including our beloved friend, Pervez Musharraf of Agra fame. And that lesson is: "Don't Outgrow Your Size, General."

■■

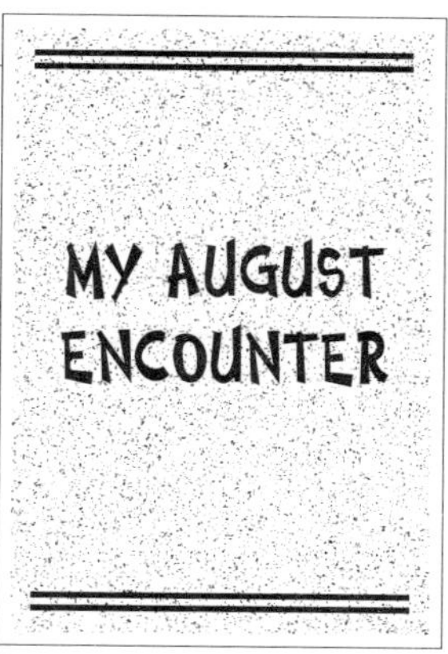

MY AUGUST ENCOUNTER

Every morning, he puts to me either of these two questions – "What is the date today? or What is the time by your watch?" I give him a reply, he thanks me, and moves away.

I don't know him, and our encounter is limited to early morning when I take my constitutional walk. He is pretty old, wears a dhoti, has a bent back, and walks slowly.

In his right hand, he carries a stick, but does not use it all the time, only when he stumbles. Or rather, when he thinks he might stumble. I have not seen him stumbling; but then I don't see him all the time.

In his left hand, he carries a bag. Made of jute. Not so pretty to look at. Rather an ordinary bag like the one people use for carrying vegetables.

He plucks flowers from the large park in Greater Kailash-II, situated a little ahead of the Don Bosco School. He does not enter the park. He cannot. There is a railing that separates the park from the pavement on which he walks. And along the railing, there is a big board which proclaims 'DLF Property, Trespassing Prohibited'.

Bushes overhang the railing. He stretches his hand towards them and plucks his flowers, mostly Marigolds, slightly orangeish. He plucks them gently and puts them in his bag, one by one.

I don't like this. I don't like anybody plucking flowers. And I don't like flowers being put in a jute bag. Why does he do so? May be for his *pooja*. May be he comes out of his residence just in search of flowers for his *pooja*...

On August 28, I gave him the wrong reply. I said it was the 29th.

"The 29th?" he asked.

"Yes," I answered. It occurred to me almost at once that I had given him the wrong date. But I was not absolutely sure myself, so I looked at my watch. I could read the time in it, but not read the date. The figures were too small and dim.

As I returned home, the calendar confirmed that I had made a mistake.

"It is the 29th today", I told him next morning. "Yesterday was the 28th. I am sorry, I did not know that."

"But I knew", said he.

"You knew?"

"Yes."

"Then why did you ask me?"

He looked at me, smiled and said: "I just wanted to talk to someone. And so I asked you. I know the date and the time and the day. They move so slowly. Don't you think so?"

■■

The young hostesses on the Thai Airways plane were as bewitching as I had always known them to be. But the first person to greet me at the Bangkok airport turned out to be a pimp. He gave me the card of one of Bangkok's massage parlours and offered that he could come and pick me up from the Hayat Rama Hotel, where I was to stay, any day, any time, convenient to me.

How did he come to know that I was to stay at Hayat Rama? Did he have any links with the World Health Organisation in Bangkok? I won't know that. But I was on a WHO assignment as a delegate from India to participate in a WHO workshop on sex education for adolescents. He pestered me quite a bit but then decided that I was not his cup of tea and moved over to some other passenger.

In my room in the hotel, after I had washed my face, I saw a small but prominent placard standing aloft on the writing desk. Welcome to Hayat Rama, it announced, walk into Blue Heaven on the third floor for a free treat. Having nothing else to do, I decided that I should avail myself of that free treat. The Thais are known for their generosity and hospitality.

A devastatingly beautiful young girl greeted me at the Blue Heaven. She conducted me to an unoccupied table and there, another angel from heaven descended and handed me a menu card listing the names of drinks. "Choose any you like," said she, "it is on the house." At first I thought that I should take Black Label with which I was familiar, but then under the influence of some sudden impulse, I opted for vodka.

Slowly, leisurely, looking all round for any acquaintance, I sipped the drink. Hardly had I finished the peg when the angel came again with her familiar tray and vodka bottle and another sparkingly clean cutglass tumbler. "On the house, Sir," she said, almost teasingly, as she poured vodka for me in that tumbler. I sipped that, too, a bit more slowly, a bit more leisurely, than the first one. But just as I finished that, the girl came again with her tray, vodka bottle and another glass tumbler.

Vodka is a strong drink. At best, I can take two pegs of it in one sitting. I declined the girl's third offer. "In that case, sir," said she, "you will have to pay for the first two pegs. Free treat means a minimum of four pegs. Less than that, you have to pay."

I don't remember how many dollars I had to shell out for my free treat. But every time I see some appealing advertisement in some paper offering something free, like an electric oven, if we buy something more expensive like a car, I start rolling my tongue on my lips.

■■

Story of a Road

During my brief stay at Kausani in the Almora district of UP (now Uttaranchal), some funny things happened. The water coming from the tap suddenly stopped. Nothing unusual about that. For, if there is one thing that can be called most erratic in its behaviour in India, it is water. It comes and goes at its will. It may be raining cats and dogs outside your house. Inside, you may not have a drop to drink. People have to make do without it for days together even at Cherapunji which gets the heaviest rainfall every year. But then behaviour of water has to be measured in relative terms. Like "Thou, too, Bruts" in Shakespeare's Julius Caesar.

Let me elaborate. The hon'ble minister was in the bathroom of the circuit house in Kausani. He was taking his bath. And just as he had finished applying soap all over his body, the water from the tap disappeared. The minister screamed. But there was none to listen. None on security duty outside the bathroom. The poor chap had no alternative but to rub the soap off his body with all the towels he could lay his hands on. The first thing that he did on emerging from the bathroom was to call the sub-divisional magistrate (SDM) on duty to maintain law and order within the vicinity of the minister's location.

The poor chap explained to the minister that that kind of thing was not unusual at Kausani. Peasants living at higher levels often cut the pipeline to divert water to their own fields. "Arrest them, arrest them all," thundered the minister.

I can't say what happened thereafter. But what I know is that one evening, the two of us staying together, in separate rooms of course, in the nearby forest rest house, saw a huge black Buick car gliding into the district board rest house down below. Hectic activities followed the arrival of that car. "Whose car is that?" I asked the SDM. "That is the car of the overseer sahib. Think of it. A petty non-gazetted official rolling in wealth." I requested him to throw some light on the gentleman's greatness. "He," whispered the SDM to me in confidence, "supervises the building of roads. The cost of constructing a road on the hills is ten times the cost of constructing the same road on the plateau. And every road he constructs anywhere, even on the plains, he shows it as a road constructed on the hills."

"Why don't you catch him?" shocked and bewildered, I asked him. "And lose my job?" said he, scratching his head, "so many before me have tried and have been pushed out of this area. You know who he is?" I did not know that and pleaded innocence. "He is," said the SDM, "known here as the Prince of Wales. He is the brother of the Chief Minister's grand-daughter's husband."

■■

Thy will be done! I whispered to the Lord and decided to beat a retreat from Patna. I had gone there by a hopping flight and was to return to Delhi the same evening. I had requested an appointment with the chief minister and he was kind enough to give me the date and time. But when I reached Patna, I did not find the chief minister there. And nobody could tell me his whereabouts. I tried the health secretary. He was away in the US as a member of a distinguished delegation of health secretaries in search of new health promotion avenues. I had sent the CM a questionnaire two weeks in advance. I had to bring out the special issue of a journal devoted to the cause of promoting family welfare. The programme was on the rocks, reasons known, in several states. I had to interview the chief ministers of those states. Bihar was one of them.

Finding neither the CM nor the health secretary in Patna, I knocked at the door of the chief secretary. He was kind enough to oblige me with a cup of tea but said at the same time, "Look, I know nothing about this hanky-panky bunkum called family planning. I am too old for it. Come again. Better luck then." Right then, someone came and informed the chief secretary that the CM had arrived. I took courage in both hands and, after taking his permission through his secretary, slipped into the room of the CM. He was equally kind. He did not throw me out. But he gave me a sonorous sermon, the sum and substance of which was that people nestling in faraway Delhi were in reality sitting on Mount Parnassus and they smelt rats everywhere. "Bihar," declared he heroically, "has no such thing as a population problem. And if there is any, I know how best to tackle it."

There was no alternative but to return. Long there-after, I ran into the same chief secretary. He had long since retired from service. “Remember that episode?” I asked him. “Of course, I do,” said he, adding smilingly, “in Bihar, they follow the *sust* (go slow), *chust* (be quick) and *durust* (that is correct) formula. I, too, learnt it and followed it responsibly as long as I was in Patna. “You know what it means? *Sust* in governance, *chust* in your own personal matters and *durust* if you follow *sust* and *chust* efficiently.”

I must say that this was long before Bihar started having twin-CMs, one de jure, one de facto, who are currently, jointly, *chustly* and *durustly*, contributing so magnificently to the “people” of the state.

■■

Every American 50 miles from his home is an expert in this or that. That is how the Green Revolution came to India. Puran Chand Batra, *Krishi Pandit*, whose farm in Rohtak I happened to visit, narrated this story. Some American agricultural experts who had descended on the agricultural university in Ludhiana descended on him also. They tried to teach Puran Chand, his father and his son, three generations of Indians, how to grow grapes in Rohtak.

Puran Chand took them to a little corner on his farm. "By Jove," exclaimed the Americans, seeing that corner, "You are already growing grapes here! Why don't you come to California and tell our blokes there how you are managing to get so much from so little?"

If family planning has flopped in India, in no small measure, this is because of the expertise the Americans have so generously bestowed on this country. In the 24-Parganas area of West Bengal, they tried to introduce the loop among Bengali women on a mass scale. Simplest, safest, surest method – they proclaimed from housetops, duly assisted by their Indian counterparts. Many women responded to them. But then some bled profusely; some developed other complications; and West Bengal rose in revolt. The Americans and their Indian counterparts took no time in folding up and running away from the scene – lock, stock and barrel.

They went to eastern UP. The rivers were in flood there. Countless villages were swallowed by them. "When the floods recede," so advised the Americans, "Why doesn't the government here raise the level of these villages?" With lots of money to throw about, they invested a million dollars or so in raising the level of some 5,000 villages. Next year, the floods became a bit more furious and all the villages thus raised were wiped out along with the rest.

In Lucknow, I saw a wonderful drama at a health conference on the diseases of the eye in villages. Roared one American expert, "Why don't you supply pressure cookers to your folks back in rural areas so that they can save their eyes from smoke?" They were ready to give aid for that. But that was ages ago when pressure cookers were not known to many even in the city of Lucknow.

Not just in India but the world over, the Americans are famous for their expertise. In Italy, they happened to visit the ruins of Rome. Not knowing that those ruins were a part of Rome's heritage, they suggested to the Italians, "You chaps over here should learn a lesson or two from New York. Over there, we have raised skyscrapers on land that was doing no good. You sure can do the same over what looks like scorched earth here."

Despite riding the high horse, despite all their idiosyncrasies, despite what they say and do, from Bill Clinton downwards, I like the Americans. But for them, the world certainly would not have been as colourful as it has come to be.

■■

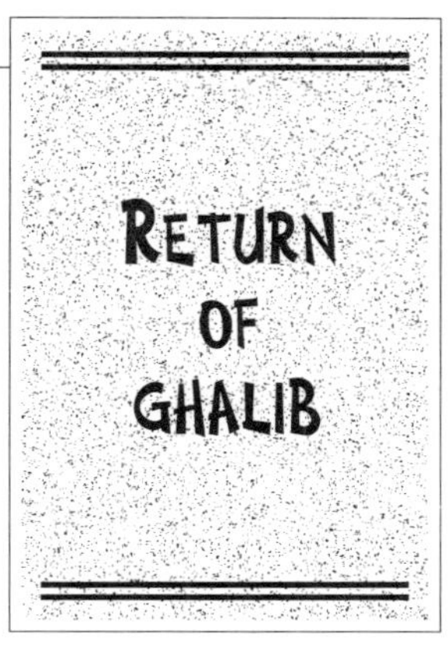

Funny things are happening to me these days. I keep on meeting great people. It is always early in the morning and it is always in the Jahanpanah city forest on the outskirts of Delhi. *Tum mere pass hote ho goyah, jab koi dusra nahin hota* (you are with me like there is none else with me). No, they don't come to me. Nor do I go to them. It just happens.

One day it is Mahatma Gandhi: I see him lost in his prayers. It is in a small cantonment called Nowsehra in the Peshawar district of NWFP. Kasturba Gandhi is sitting by his side. "Is this woman his sister?" an aged Pathan asks me. "No," I reply, "it is his wife." "*Khuda ka ghazab* (calamity from God)," says the Pathan, "*Malang baba biwi ko saath le kar jaga-jaga ghoomta hae* (moves about from place to place along with his wife)." *Malang Baba* (one who has renounced the world) is how Gandhiji is affectionately referred to by Pathans.

Another day, it is Jawaharlal Nehru! I see him sitting in his room in the South Block, clipping his nails. Security people try to prevent me from barging in like that. I give them right and left and walk in. "Where have you descended from?" Panditji asks me, amazed. I break down. "My parents, brother and sisters are stranded in Peshawar," I sob, "and I want you to get them evacuated." Jawaharlal gets up, puts his hands on my shoulders like a father and walks out of the room with me and saying, "We have requisitioned BOAC planes to evacuate people from distant places. Nothing will happen to your parents. We are doing our best."

On yet another day, it is Sarojini Naidu: I see her examining the arrangements they have made for the stay of Mahatma Gandhi in the Bhangi Colony in Delhi. She seems happy to find everything spick and span and I hear her whispering to herself, "If only the Mahatma knew how much it costs us to make life simple for him."

And on yet another day, I see Indira Gandhi stranded with her two children at an exhibition called "Our Heritage," in the Cross Maidan in Bombay. She is nobody. But she is the Prime Minister's daughter and as such everybody. Jawaharlal is held up viewing exhibits in some other pavilion. It is noon-time. And it is April, the worst month in Bombay. The sun is blowing fire below. "Madam," I ask Indira Gandhi, "would you care to come into the shade in our pavilion?" She walks in along with Rajiv and Sanjay. "Would you like to have some water?" I ask her. She nods her head in assent. And I discover that there is no water available in the pavilion.

I find Lal Bahadur Shastri, too, roaming about in the forest. He is a minister in Jawaharlal's Cabinet. There is the Commonwealth Prime Ministers' Conference in London.

Jawaharlal is unable to go there. He asks Shastriji to represent him at the conference. Shastriji agrees but tells Panditji that it would be very cold in London and he has no overcoat. Jawaharlal offers him his own coat and Shastriji tries it, and gets lost in it.

Lately, I have been meeting another gentleman, rather frequently. No, he is not from ages gone by. He has just come to occupy the pinnacles of glory. I always find him clad in a lovely dhoti and kurta, sitting on a big rock all alone. The face seems as familiar as that of Jawaharlal. I don't have to tax my mind to recognise him. Once upon a time, not long ago, he used to be called Atal Behari Vajpayee. "What are you doing here early in the morning?" I ask him. He looks at me and murmurs, "*Ishq ne, Ghalib, Nikamma kar diya; warna ham bhi admi thay kam ke* (Love has ruined me, oh Ghalib; otherwise, I too, was a man of some substance.)"

■■

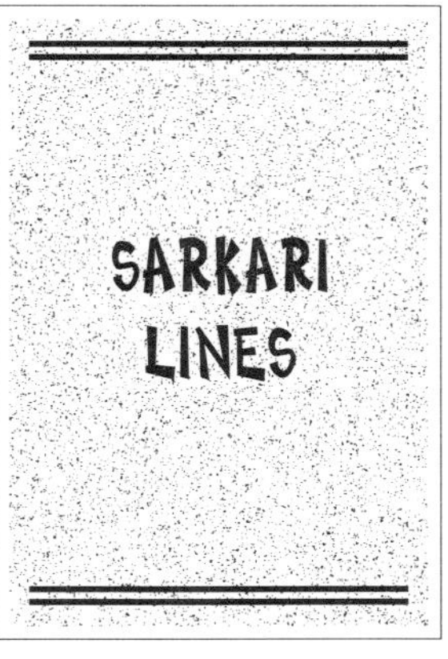

SARKARI LINES

We may grumble about the price of our newspaper. But we seldom have cause to grumble about the manner in which it comes to us. The boy who brings it on his cycle is an expert marksman. From down below, he throws it up on to the balcony of our flat on the first floor – or, be it, the residents on the second floor. He seldom misses his mark. Sometimes, only sometimes, if the paper falls down, he chucks it up again. And it reaches where he intends it to go.

We have faith in him. We look for him eagerly each morning and he seldom lets us down. As a rule, he comes regularly. And he is almost always punctual. He practises no dishonesty. And what he gives to us is pure and unadulterated; I mean, as it comes to him from the office or agent of the newspaper. As a middleman, he does not indulge in anything hanky-panky.

He is also very considerate. When along with my daily papers, I get some periodicals also, he comes up to my second-storey flat and delivers them to me personally. When it rains, he does the same. He has never delivered a wet or torn paper to me. During the rainy season, he wraps his bundles in thick plastic sheets; he may get drenched himself, but he does not allow the papers to get wet.

Unlike the man who operates cable network in our complex and gives no receipt for what he collects from his customers, the newspaper boy operates in the open. He lists in the bill all that he gives and brings the bill to us personally, late in the evening and, generally, not on the first of the month. He knows that people don't like to part with their money on the first, and first thing in the morning at that. He gives a proper receipt for what he takes.

How much does he get for what he does? I knew that it was part-time side activity, confined to the early hours of the morning only. Nobody could live by it alone. But I was surprised to learn from the boy that he was able to make over Rs 1,500 each month. And that is after giving commission or whatever it is called to the agency for which he works.

What does he do during the rest of the day? I asked him one January evening. He named a certain Government organisation in which he is employed as a messenger on an ad hoc basis. The organisation deals with the public and is notorious for its indifference to it, as well as for alleged malpractices. "How is it," I put it to him, "that while you are so good, your department has such a bad reputation?"

"Sarkari work is sarkari," he replied smilingly, "it runs along sarkari lines."

■■

Ask anyone in England how many kids he has. For the rest of your stay in that country, the man will not speak to you. Put the same question to a bloke in Chandigarh and he will say something like this: "Two sons, one doctor, one engineer, both settled in the United States, three daughters, one living in Canada, one in Bombay and one in Calcutta. All doing well, with your kind blessings and by the grace of God." No hesitation, no compunction. He will tell you gladly all that you may need to know.

In whatever part of India we may be living, we are a nation full of bonhomie. I find marvellous evidence of this early every morning as I visit the Jahanpanah city forest on the outskirts of Delhi. Right in the beginning, there is a group of some 20-30 men, all past their prime time, doing one-two-three. One man comes out and shouts one. All raise their arms. He shouts two. They bring the arms to shoulder level. He shouts three. They bring the arms further down.

The drill goes on for 10 minutes or so. No need for arms to synchronise. Sometimes when the dril-master shouts one, someone's arm may not go up at all. Everybody rushes to his aid. Elderly people, they call themselves senior citizens. The drill-master changes turn by turn. On Sundays, they bring tea in flasks from home and have a sort of picnic there.

Move on to the park adjoining this lovely scene. A yogic maharishi is teaching yoga to women, mostly grandmothers, wanting to shed off a bit of weight or get rid of some pain in the knee-joints. They bring their own *durees* from home and do their exercise lying on them. The maharishi knows their *posheeda* (secret) problem as well — how to get younger and look lovelier day by day. He helps them in tackling that, too, to the best of his expertise.

Both men and women know who is who. They are all on visiting terms. So are the ones, mostly males, forming a different group, who, after finishing their constitutional walk, sit on a culvert in the middle of the forest. They discuss things of yore, as well as things of today, from Lalloo of Hum Log to Laloo of Bihar.

"Have you taken your sarbitrate before coming here in the morning?" asks one. "No," replies the one to whom the question is directed. "I went to my cardiologist yesterday and he said that sarbitrate should be taken only when there is a heart attack. It should not be taken every day."

"How will you know?" buts in another, equally experienced in the matter of heart attacks and sarbitrate, "when the heart attack comes? Who will give your sarbitrate to you at that time? And on what address will he send it to you if you pop off per chance?"

A heated discussion follows on when to take sarbitrate – daily, before the heart attack or after the heart attack. "*Chhaddo badshaho* (leave it at that)," the apparently most experienced among them all cuts it short, "for 10 years, I have been invariably carrying my sarbitrate in my pocket. I have never needed it. But I keep it nevertheless. Who knows who else may need it when and where?"

■■

In the early part of twentieth century, when Prithvi Raj Kapoor left Peshawar for Bombay, everybody said to his mother that she had lost her son to sin. For Bombay (now Mumbai) was known as "Paap ki Nagri" (City of Sin). So was Lahore, to a certain extent. In Lahore, I discovered that the likes of me coming from Peshawar were downright rogues and ruffians. And those from Jhang, from where comes my wife as also Heer of Heer Ranjha fame, were plain nitwits and nincompoops.

As the time passed, many other discoveries about the great reputation of our towns and cities I made. For instance, all the bloody fools in the world came from Shikarpur in Sindh. And all the geniuses from Bengal. Intellectuals were the monopoly of Madras, and filthy language that of Rohtak, Hisar, Gurgaon and Rewari.

Leaving aside all other places, let me tell you something about Ballia. That town in eastern UP was as much famous for its great role in the freedom struggle as for everything that was wrong in the world. And that included what was called Balliatic by wags in the coffee house in Lucknow.

It is very difficult to define what Balliatic means. Tomfoolery would probably be the one word to describe it. In the sophisticated culture of Lucknow, anybody saying something funny or stupid was labelled as Balliatic. It is said that such was the reputation of Ballia that during the British days, no British ICS officer wanted to be posted there as Deputy Commissioner. That was considered to be a punishment. One young officer who had freshly come from England and was exiled to Ballia retaliated by spending all his time in his big bungalow there and doing nothing.

The town was on fire. Electricity and telegraph poles had been pulled down by revolutionaries, and even cats and dogs had turned hostile. Buses were burnt, railway tracks blown up, buildings bombed and everything that smacked of British rule smashed into bits. The gentleman sent no report to Lucknow. Telegrams came from there asking him to set things right. He threw them in the waste-paper basket. Despite phone calls and reminders, threats of dire action and things like that, he remained unruffled.

Finally, seeing things going from bad to worse and getting no report from him, the Home Secretary called him to Lucknow. Pulled up badly, the bloke hit him back. "Do your worst," said he to the Home Secretary, "I am already in Ballia. What else can you do against me?"

When someone talks to me these days of the quarrels and quibbles our great leaders are having among themselves, calling one another names like kids in school do, and asks me, "aren't they concerned about the plight of the people who have chosen them?" I feel like telling him, "never mind, what else can they do to us? We are already in Ballia."

I don't say that. For Ballia, I am sure, must have by now left its great Balliatic reputation far behind it.

■■

NO MORE LETTERS TO PAKISTANI FRIENDS

If you happen to have any friend in Pakistan, for God's sake, don't write any letter to him. He may run into trouble. Your letter may fall into hands that may throttle his throat.

Looks, we have fallen back to the days immediately after Partition. At that time, having been thrown out of Peshawar, my home-town, I committed the blunder of joining lots of other writers in trying to build bridges between India and the new country that had been caved out of India's body.

I wrote no letters to anyone. I scribbled middles. And in one of these middles, I talked of the nobility of a Pathan dhobi living in the village of Tehkal, close to my alma mater, Islamia College. His name was Ayub.

I was not in Peshawar in September, 1947, when our locality, mohalla Kakaran, was attacked by thousands of our neighbours joined by those from the tribal areas and the armed constables of the local police. My father, who had retired as an army officer just a month earlier, had fought against the hordes, along with the rest of the mohalla people. He was wounded.

The whole lot, the people of the mohalla, such of them as had survived the holocaust, were taken to the Balasar Fort after the attack. There, none of those whom they might have done some good some other day came to offer a bit of sympathy to them. That was the one thing they would have valued. They could not have gone back to their mohalla. It had been reduced to ashes.

It was the worst of times. Independence had come. And yet it was the darkest moment in India's history. If India had to be partitioned, why could it not be partitioned peacefully? Stupid question. Too late to raise it.

In the midst of darkness, in the midst of darkness everywhere, someone always comes to give you a ray of hope. That is the Lord's way. The Lord does not want darkness to engulf us completely. He has to run the world. He has given to man two sides – one that takes him upwards towards Him, and the other that pulls him down into some fathomless pit.

Ayub, the dhobi, belonged to the category that takes man upwards. He came all the way from his village Tehkal, to the Balasar Fort to offer to those whose clothes he had washed all his life some words of remorse, some words of sympathy. How did he manage to come there? Did he have someone known among the constables guarding the fort? No one knows.

The nobility of that gesture I had tried to capture in my middle in the sixties, following another skirmish with Pakistan. Kind of the Indian Express that it carried that middle.

What happened then? Binod Rao, the Express Editor in Bombay, showed me a letter addressed to Frank Moraes, the Chief Editor, by the Pakistan High Commissioner in New Delhi. The letter accused me of being an irresponsible writer.

The Deputy Commissioner of Peshawar, so said the letter, had located Ayub. And even though Ayub acknowledged that he used to wash the clothes of some Hindus and Sikhs in Peshawar, he denied having ever visited the Balasar Fort.

God knows what they must have done to Ayub. They must have punished him for the sin of his nobility. And so I say, notwithstanding its latest perfidy in Kargil, go on building bridges with Pakistan. But for God's sake, write no more letters to friends over there. Look at what has happened to Najam Sethi!

■■

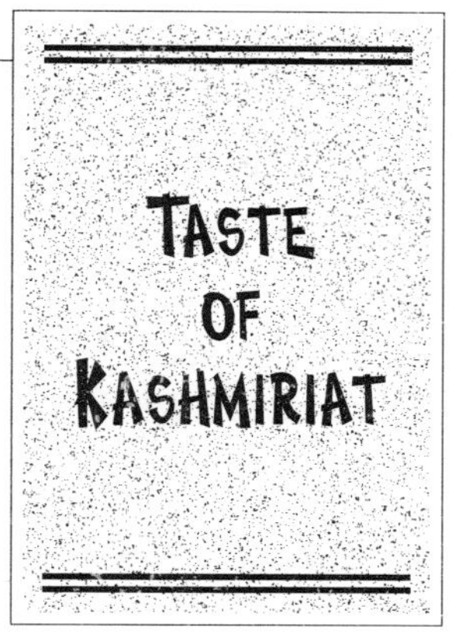

What is Kashmiriat? How do we define it? Is it a capsule version of the kind of togetherness that prevails in India? What is this togetherness? I won't attempt an answer to those questions. I would rather live the answer, like the tall *khansama* in the circuit house in Srinagar where I used to stay whenever I went to Kashmir in days gone by.

"This *chugha* (long robe), this *kangri* (small earthen *angithi*)," he said to me one night, after dinner, as he served me green tea in my room, "are all our inheritance. Our *abba-o-ajdad* (forefathers) have bequeathed them to us. As if these were not enough, Delhi has now also made its contribution. It has sent its T.V. If people had not turned *kayal* (lazy), what else they could have turned out to be?"

I wanted to ask him why he had not served *gushtaba* (Kashmiri meat and egg delicacy) to the honourable professor from the Aligarh University who was also staying in the circuit house, in a different room, of course. We were not known to each other.

He had served *gushtaba* to me as part of my dinner. And he had also offered me another helping which I had declined. But when the Aligarh man asked for it, he had said that *gushtaba* was not available. The distinguished professor had looked at my plate wistfully. He had surveyed the number of mutton pieces in it. These had probably appeared to be more than what had been given to him. He had asked for a bit more mutton. The *khansama* had said that, too, was not available.

Earlier, in the morning, I had been given my cornflakes with a small jug of milk. That was followed by toasts and two half-fried eggs. The scholar from Aligarh was straightaway served toasts and eggs. "Where are my cornflakes? he had asked the *khansama*. "No cornflakes," the latter had said, "all *khallas* (finished)."

I knew that that was not the case. He had opened a fresh packet of cornflakes and taken it back after serving the stuff to me. "But how come," the professor had protested, "that you have given cornflakes to this gentleman? Am I being charged less for my food here? Aren't the rates the same for all? Why this discrimination?"

The *khansama* had frowned but given no answer. At tea-time in the evening, I asked him why he had treated the Aligarh gentleman so differently. I had known him for years. He was a good man. He had always behaved nicely with all people.

"I don't like that fellow," said he, without a bit of hesitation, "I don't like the likes of him. He is a Muslim. So am I. But I don't have to proclaim to the whole world that I am a Muslim. I say my prayers five times a day. That is enough for me."

"He is the type," he went on, as if I had blown some air on some fire burning within him, "that divides brother from brother, Hindu Dhar from Muslim Dhar, Hindu Bhatt from Muslim Bhatt, Hindu Pandit from Muslim Pandit. I might have asked him whether God was Hindu or Muslim. But there was no use. What is the good of putting to shame those who have no sense of shame?"

The man didn't answer my question why he had not served *gushtaba* etc. to the gentleman from Aligarh. But it occurred to me that the great scholar must have said something to him that was repugnant to all that he had cherished as part of his Kashmiriat. And simple as he was, he had hit him back in his own way by denying to him what he was otherwise legitimately entitled to.

■■

Having died, Nikka never wanted to come back to life. He had become so used to basking in the glory of his situation. Left to himself, he would have continued to rest in peace. But, then the phone call came and it threw up a promise he could not resist.

How did Nikka die? We shall come to that later. Let us begin from the beginning.

Nikka was born in 1960 in a prosperous family of farmers in the town of Khialpur in the Dreamabad district of Punjab, bordering Holyland. A bright boy, after his schooling, he was admitted to the IIT in Kharagpur for B.E. in mechanical engineering.

He had no dearth of money. Nor of love, from home or within the institute, where in the third year of his studies everybody knew that he and Nikki, his classmate, were destined to spend the rest of their lives together.

As their affair blossomed, the frequency of Nikka's letters back home declined. His worried father sent his elder brother to Kharagpur to find out what was what. The latter did not find Nikka there. He sent him again. The result was the same.

Someone said that Nikka had become a drug-addict. From Dreamabad came the news that he had turned into a drug-trafficker, then a smuggler of arms, then a terrorist. Gradually more things came to light. Nikka had fallen out with his gang leader and had formed a gang of his own. He had also become its Lt. General.

His gang had emerged as the most dreaded one in the entire Dreamabad area and was responsible for several killings and blowing up of rail-tracks. The government had announced a reward of Rs 10 lakh for the capture of Nikka, dead or alive.

And then one day in 1991, Nikka died. There were so many stories about the circumstances of his death. Some said that he had been killed by the Lt. General of the gang to which he had once belonged. Some others said that he had been killed in an encounter with the police.

There was also a rumour that there was no real encounter but only a faked one and that Nikka had indeed been captured alive by the police and tortured to death and the Human Rights Organisation as well as Amnesty International had taken up his case at various fora.

Nikka was known to be far too brave to commit suicide. In any case, his heart-broken parents wanted to have his body. It was not given to them. They were told that it had been taken away by other members of his gang.

Nikka's bhog ceremony was performed in Khialpur. It was attended by several political leaders and the commanders and Lt. Generals of all the principal gangs operating in the area.

Having died, Nikka did not want to return to life. But when the phone call came, he dashed from New York to Khialpur. His parents bowed before the Lord. His brothers lifted him on their shoulders. As they all sat down after the initial euphoria, the following things came to light.

Nikka's brother had gone to Gorakhpur in UP and not to Kharagpur in West Bengal. After completing their studies, Nikka and Nikki had moved over to USA. Nikka had not informed his parents about their marriage because Nikki was a Bengali girl and Nikka feared that she might not be accepted by his family.

"What brings you here now?" asked his brothers.

"The money that was collected for building my memorial," answered Nikka, adding, "the phone call said that from Canada and USA alone, more than a million dollars had come. Where is that money?"

"A lot had come," said his father, "that is what we had heard. But since we were all mourning your death, we did not bother to know who had taken it away." ■■

Countless memories are associated with the city of my birth, Peshawar. Right now, when everybody is talking about missiles, as if man has discovered the final formula for his survival in them "from here to eternity," these have pushed everything else aside.

A mile or so from the Islamia College, my alma mater, on the road to the Khyber Pass, there used to be a bridge over what might once have been a river. The Hindukush mountains, through which the Khyber Pass runs, were far away from the sweep of monsoons. It seldom rained there on the rocky terrains. Rains came only in winter and that, too, for a brief spell. God knows in what age the river had come into being. In any case, in the forties, it was all river-bed and nothing more.

And yet people crossed it through the concrete bridge over it. They never went down to tread the river-bed. For it was the common belief that the bed was studded with the bones of their ancestors who had died fighting against the invaders from the north. What were indeed stones and pebbles did look like crushed bones. Someone had set afloat the story that these in reality were crushed bones. And Pathans being Pathans, they believed in such stories easily. In any case, they were not prepared to trample under foot what might have been the last remains of their own forefathers and *their* forefathers.

Nobody talked of Mohd. Ghauri and Mahmood Ghaznvi in those parts then. But history books did tell little kids that they and the like of them were the ones fighting against whom their forefathers and forefathers' fathers had died. I do not know whether any hostile feelings were there in the minds of the Pathans against

Ghauri, Ghaznvi, Halakoo and others. But invaders were invaders. No city was named after them. Nor was any place where Ghauri and Ghaznvi might have fought against the local people turned into a *ziarat* (place of pilgrimage).

Opposite to my college was a village. Some of our Pathan bearers in the hostels came from there. "Hari Singh Nalwa *raghle de*" (Hari Singh Nalwa has come) – that was the threat Pathan mothers used to put their children to sleep. They were still afraid of Hari Singh Nalwa, or maybe they were not afraid and they only wanted to instil the fear of Nalwa in the minds of their kids. Nalwa was Maharaja Ranjit Singh's general. He had conquered those parts. Whether or not he was a terror, I can't say. But "*Nalwa raghle de*" was like telling people that the Lord's fury was about to visit them. This was not just the case with that one village. The fear of Nalwa was widespread.

As we would come back to our college from evening walks, an ancient Pathan, standing on the college side of the bridge, would invariably offer a red rose to Haddow Harris, our Scot professor of English literature. Harris used to accompany us. That was his way of taking his class: just three or four of us. Harris would gratefully accept the rose from the old Pathan and give him a four-anna coin for it.

Subah-dam murghe-e chaman ba gul-e no-khasta guft; naaz kam kun kae bas-a chun to dar-in bagh shiguft (early in the morning, the bird in the garden said to the freshly-opened flower; don't be so coquettish, for many like you have blossomed in this garden) – that old Persian couplet comes to my mind as I think of the rose that the old man used to give to Haddow Harris and as I find myself intrigued by all this talk of missiles which Pakistan threatens to use against India. Everything else fades away, but those three memories remain.

■■

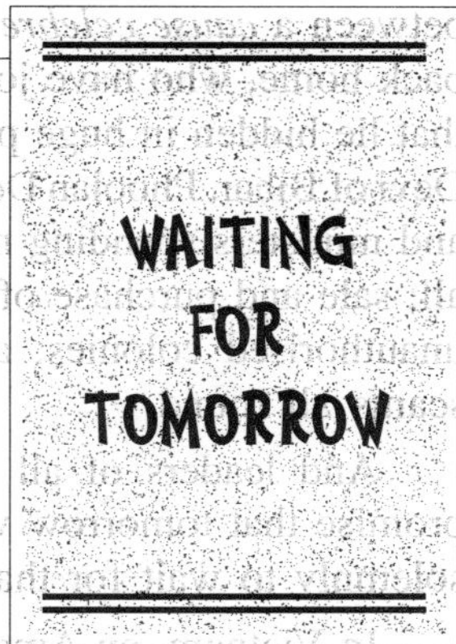

WAITING FOR TOMORROW

What the dickens is happening? Except for my early morning walk, I have stopped moving out of my house for I have the fear that one of those monstrous hearse vans that move on the strength of a legitimate licence from the Delhi Transport Undertaking might mistake me for a dead person and carry me straight to the Nigambodh Ghat.

I used to go to the India International Centre, the American Library and the British Council. I have stopped doing that. For I have the fear that my little car might be overrun by some flying saucer descended on Mother Earth in the garb of that bloke called the pedestrian who jumps from one side of the road to the other.

I would say, though, that he is highly in demand. Because the likes of him constitute what are known as 'vote-banks'. This party or that, he is himself a lost man. For he knows not the difference between tweedledums and tweedledees.

He has lived on promises long enough to forget who is who. All that he remembers is that a thin old man called Mahatma Gandhi had obtained for him what is called the right to vote, and he has to exercise that right regularly to show to the world at large that he is wise and patriotic enough.

So I remain confined within the four walls of my little flat. And I collect every morning the three or four newspapers that that pointsman called the newspaper boy throws so accurately from down below to hit the door of my flat, 36 steps up. Like missiles, those newspapers come. And like missiles, they explode the moment they hit their target. No, not the door, but poor me who reads them.

For what do we find in them? Bill Clinton and his antics, and Tony Blair standing by him like a buddy who knows well the kinship between a *cause celebre* and destiny; this Yadav and that Yadav, back home, who have joined hands to salvage us from gangsters that lie hidden in huge piles of fodder and things like that; Rabri Devi of Bihar, Phoolan Devi of UP; their Excellencies the governors and ministers spending more on tea and travel than on health for all; sale and purchase of legislators; unauthorised defections like unauthorised colonies; a kidnapping here, a murder there, and scams all round.

And leaders of all hues and shades holding before us the promise that tomorrow will certainly be better, and expecting us solemnly to wait for that tomorrow.

In Vietnam, an American soldier, tired and fed up with war, lies under a tree, his arms and bags scattered around him. A photographer from *Life* approaches him. "What are you waiting for?" asks the photographer. "Tomorrow," flows the reply from the parched lips of the soldier.

That was decades ago. Is that war still on? Is that tomorrow of that soldier's dream still eluding us? How do we define it?

I am confused.

■■

It is no ordinary watch that tells time alone. As a matter of fact, ordinarily it does not tell time at all. Most of the time, it is itself asleep, lying in the locker of my almirah. It tells time only when I take it out, wind it and tie it on my wrist or keep it in my pocket.

Long long ago, during World War II, my father, an Army Officer, had bought it from an Army canteen for Rs 62. Thereafter, it 'saw' action in Burma and then in the battle of Peshawar that took place at the time of partition. My father had it on his wrist while fighting against the tribal hordes and the local hooligans who had invaded our locality, **mohalla** Kakaran, in Peshawar city, on Sept. 7, 1947.

He lost everything in that battle, including his shoes and his specs, but the watch remained intact, tied securely on his wrist. On coming to India, he wore it as long as he lived. Thereafter, in 1962, my mother passed it on to me and I gave it to my younger sister.

She wore it as long as she needed it and then it went to my elder daughter. Fashions had changed. This watch, called Prima Sawar, had to be wound every day. Automatic watches had come in the market. So had battery-operated quartz – Seikos and Citizens, HMTs and Titans. The days of watches that had to be wound had gone like the days of the fountain-pens which were replaced by ballpoints and the days of the black and white TV sets which had surrendered before their coloured cousins.

A watch falls down from your hand, a Seiko or Citizen, and it goes silent. It goes silent also when the battery on whose strength its needles move gets weak. I have several such weak-hearted watches. Their repairs cost a fortune. On each of them, I have spent a lot. When all let me down, I take out my father's Prima Sawar, wind it set the time and move about without any fear of it betraying me in any manner at any point.

It has never let me down. For, as I said, it is no ordinary watch. Though more than fifty years old and most of the time asleep, when I take it out and wind it, it shows me time, correct to the dot. So many memories are associated with this watch. It is part of my heritage.

■■

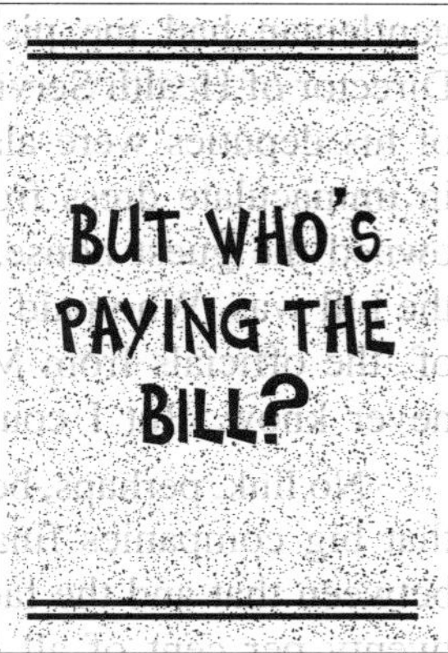

Whenever the seven-year-itch to breathe some fresh air away from India grips you terribly, attach yourself to the coattails of the Director General of Health Services (DGHS). Wangle a trip to some of the places he visits. He has VIP patients suffering from some pain everywhere. He gets royal treatment, limousines, guest houses and all that on the house. As a part of his retinue, you get the same."

That was the advice a joint secretary in the ministry of health gave me a long time ago. The DG was a famous orthopaedic surgeon. He was a member of health advisory committees, whatever that means, in several other countries. As a result, he was more often found abroad than in Delhi. I could never get the opportunity to latch on to the DG's entourage. More influential people always managed to beat me to it. Nevertheless, once, accidentally, I had the privilege to travel with one of his deputies, designated marketing executive (ME), to Mumbai. "Where will you stay?" he asked me on the plane. "With my brother-in-law on the Malabar Hill," I answered honestly. "On the way, why not have a drink with me in the guest house?" he threw the temptation at me. I could not escape. Next came an invitation to lunch at the Taj. How could he afford to visit these expensive places? It was not for me to question. I succumbed.

The guest house was a posh affair, stolen from the Arabian Nights. It belonged to a well-known drug manufacturing company. "How much do you have to pay for this?" I asked the gentleman. "Nothing," said he, "it is a small courtesy. How are you placed tomorrow?"

I was well placed. I had to see the rough-cuts of some half a dozen films on health in the Films Division. From there, the gentleman had me picked up and transported to the Taj. The Director of Health Services, Government of Maharashtra; and two of his deputies were also present at the lunch. So was a bigwig in immaculate dress from the same pharmaceutical concern that owned the guest house. It was not for me to inquire how much the bill was. Who paid it? Of course, it was not the ME. Nor any of the officials from Maharashtra. Someone else. Who? I could never know. But I could guess.

No link, perhaps, between that nauseating episode and the fact that big companies finance officials' trips abroad. Nor any link between that and the factoid doled out by the WHO recently that twenty per cent of all drugs being sold in India are fake.

■■

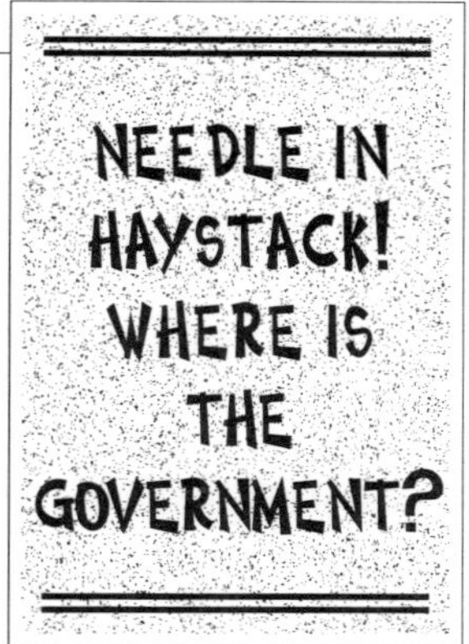

Four doctors (all females, pardon me, ladies) were sitting in their cabins with fingers crossed and lots and lots of patients waiting outside. That was the scene in a CGHS dispensary I happened to visit during the election epidemic in the third week of November. I wanted to show some part of my anatomy, which could not be exposed to a lady doctor, to one of the male members of the species. But no such bloke was visible.

Have all men been pushed out of the medical profession? Not, for me to raise that kind of question. I walked into the cabin of one of the glorious ladies and explained to her that something had erupted where it ought not to have erupted. Referred to Safdarjung Hospital – she scribbled my prescription. "Why to the hospital?" I asked naturally, "It is a minor thing and can surely be taken care of here through a course of anti-biotics." "Where are the anti-biotics?" was her counter-question, "For that matter, where is the government?"

She informed me that drugs indented long time back had not been received in the dispensary. I walked into the room of the chief medical officer. She corroborated her junior's statement, adding smilingly, "The government has not been in existence for long. Patients come and go wringing their hands in despair." And she added, by the way, so she said, "You, too, were holding a senior position in the governments. Why don't you rap it? And what were you doing when you were yourself in position?"

That was long, long ago, and if 1 remember correctly, the government did exist at that time. How else was I getting my salary? Anyhow, be that as it may be, in 1981, on leaving the government, as I had inherited it, I shifted to my own little flat in the Tara Apartments in Alaknanda. There was no proper road from GK-II to where I had landed then.

A road came much later. That is the custom in India. Towns are built. Roads emerge later. It is unlike property dealers who emerge before property emerges.

Within my memory and right under my nose, all the well known rivers and mountains of India have emerged in the area. These include Yamuna, Narmada, Ganga, Gangotri, Kaveri, Nilgiri and Shivalik. Someone in that glorious organisation called the DDA must have been a great lover of India's glorious heritage that he gave these glorious names to the clusters that have come up in the area in the form of what are known as self-financing flats. But while he christened them thus, he forgot to give to the flats two of their vital but not self-financing needs, electricity and water, in the measure required.

What happens now? The same as happened to me in the CGHS dispensary.

Electricity supply fails here more often than it is in position. Water needs the support of booster pumps to reach up to where you live. You have to caress and cajole Delhi Vidyut Board and the Water Supply Undertaking, the all-important wings of the thing called government before these start fluttering. But then, as the lady doctors told me in that dispensary of which I am an alleged beneficiary, where is the government?

■■

Standing in the queue in the income tax office in Mayur Bhavan in New Delhi, waiting for my turn to file the IT return, I got the feeling as if I was sitting in one of those Dakota planes, called war-horses, in which I used to fly between Calcutta and Gauhati in days gone by. With dozens of pedestal fans, placed here and there, blowing at full speed, competing with the noise that came from the sunk breasts of those who once upon a time were GOI's "Think Tanks", occupying high positions, nothing could have been more exasperating.

It was the 25th of June, the first day to file the return. As a rule, I always file my return personally and on the first day. My son rebukes me for not engaging a chartered accountant. "Why spend money on something which your mother can do better?" I tell him, "after all, she holds an hons. degree in mathematics signed by Mian Sir Fazal Hussain himself."

Mian Sir Fazal Hussain was the Vice-Chancellor of the Panjab University in our times, times before 1947, times when Hindus were Hindus, Sikhs were Sikhs, Muslims were Muslims, all gentlemen, no terrorists, no mujahideen among them.

To be on the right side of the law, I had deposited a sum of Rs 3,000 into the bank as advance tax. Subsequent calculations revealed that that was more than what I ought to have deposited. In plain words, the IT Department had to return to me a sum of Rs 585 as refund.

Good of them that for the elderly, now-called bazurgs, they had separate counters and that, too, in alphabetical order. My name beginning with V, I stood at the counter intended for those between M and Z.

More than an hour passed and yet my turn did not come. "If we can wait a little more," my wife encouraged me, "they are giving refund cheques to others on the spot. We, too, might get ours."

Happy are those who file no returns. Look at the chatwallahs. Aren't they earning more than what we get? Any fellow who sells monkey-nuts in the bazars of Delhi makes more than what the government pays us as our pension. Do they file any returns? We seem to be the only bloody fools who pay our taxes and on top of that stand in queues for hours.

I heard those remarks and similar other commentaries from the GOI's ex-bigwigs. "Waiting for your turn to get the refund?" a kindly gentleman, apparently a deputy commissioner of income tax, came up and put the question to me. I nodded my head. He must have put that question to many others. "How long have you been waiting?" he asked me. "Nearly two hours," I replied. He walked up to the official checking the claims, talked to him and came back to me. "Just a few minutes more, Sir," said he, "you are fourth on the list."

My turn came. And lo and behold, the official handling my case gave me a cheque for exactly Rs 585, the amount I had claimed. "Was my assessment correct?" I asked him. "I don't know, Sir," replied he, "as rule, we don't check the refund claims of those in your income bracket. We take them to be correct."

■■

MUJAHIDEEN OF PESHAWAR

But for brief intermittent breaks in Shimla, Ambala and Ferozepore, necessitated by my father's army postings I spent the first 24 years of my life among the mujahideen of Peshawar, Bannu and Nowshehra. Of course, in those days, those fellows were not known as mujahideen. They were plain looters and murderers.

My grandfather used to tell me that every Friday, they would come to Peshawar from the adjoining tribal areas and loot Hindu and Sikh shops there. Sometimes, they would try to loot houses as well. That was the reason why every house on its top fifth storey had a morcha. Men would go up there and shower bullets on the mujahideen down. That would drive them away.

In earlier times, they had to be paid *jazia* (religious tax) too. "Pay them their *jazia* and they would go back home. For they come not so much to kill Hindus and Sikhs as to loot them. Killing was done only when there was resistance against looting."

Looting apart, what else kept them going? Manufacture of illicit arms in underground factories and trafficking in illicit drugs like hashish and cocaine, locally grown and coming from Afghanistan. In these enterprises, one of their principal accomplices was the tehsildar of Landikotal, the last railway station on the Northern Railway, four miles this side of the Afghan border. He was one of the richest persons in those areas. And he was duly protected by the British for he was the one who used to keep an eye on the khasedars in the villages around. Those khasedars were appointed by the British, on the recommendation of the Political Agent, as village constables on Rs 10 per month. One of their principal responsibilities was to see that the roads in their areas were kept safe for the movement of troops.

In my days, in the forties, I could see the mujahideen standing on the benches in cinema houses during interval and ogling women, mostly prostitutes, sitting in the gallery. Not just ogling them but also indulging in perverted sex, all by themselves. They would do that unmindful of any norms known to civilisation, including perhaps their own brand of it. The Pathan gatekeepers would see that but adopt the "couldn't care less" kind of attitude towards the ugly spectacle.

When did those fellows assume the high-sounding denomination of jehadis, mujahids or mujahideen? Was it in 1947 when they invaded Baramula and other places in Kashmir and raped Muslim girls en masse? Or was it when they joined the Afghans in throwing the Russians out of Afghanistan?

Did they know the holy Koran? Its meanings? Its noble principles? Principles common to all religions. Did they know how to read the holy Koran? I can't answer that. But on the way to my alma mater, Islamia College, Peshawar, there was a tiny mosque. Returning from the cantonment on their cycles, one day some students stopped there to quench their thirst. Out came a jehadi with a dagger in hand. "This is not a piao (drinking water booth) or your father's house", said he, "that you have come here to drink water. Go away before I pierce the dagger through your stomach".

The man was a gambler. He along with his gang was using the mosque as a gambling den.

■■

Every time I read about the death of a flying officer in an aircraft accident, my mind goes bock to that dark December morning in Peshawar in 1946 when I was a witness to one such tragedy. It occurred not far away from my Alma Mater, Islamia College, where I was doing my postgraduation.

Our poetry teacher, Haddow Harris, had not come. We were basking in the sun on the lawn outside the class-room. Suddenly we saw a solitary aircraft indulging in acrobatics above us.

It was fascinating to watch it. Sailing fast across the sky like a shooting star, piercing furiously through its bosom, disappearing into the yonder beyond, re-emerging, plunging downwards, moving upwards again, steadying itself, taking topsy-turvy turns – it held us spell-bound.

The crash took place in the twinkling of an eye. The plane dived deeper than was stipulated and hit the ground.

We rushed to the accident site. It seemed so near but then turned out to be a mile away. There we saw the wreckage spread over a vast area and smoke coming from the pilot's body, burnt beyond recognition. From the nearby R.A.F. Flying School, a few British officers had already reached the spot. They were all standing silently there. We stood a little away.

Nothing could be done. An unbearable silence pervaded the scene. And then, God knows why, looking at the RAF officers, I uttered that ignoble sentence: "Was he an Indian?" It was like throwing a stone on a dead body. An RAF officer looked at me scornfully and darted back: "He was a man."

Yes, he was a man. And I have not been able to forgive myself for that awful sentence I uttered unintentionally that dark December morning in 1946. Unto this day, I do not know to what nationality the dead pilot belonged.

The episode and my own role in it came back to me devastatingly fresh once again in the second half of September as I read about the death of Flying Lieut. Dawra in Ladakh. He was showing to a Press party assembled at Leh how the Indian boys were protecting the Indian sky against possible intrusions from across. In the process, his MiG 21 hit the high mountains and he lost his life.

How many of them – soldiers, sailors, airmen – have died at the altar of freedom in the conflicts inflicted on us in 1962, 1965, 1971, and in the periods before, between and thereafter?

Somewhere in Aksai Chin, they have raised an epithet on a spot where several Indian soldiers died in 1962. It says in the words of an English poet:

How can a man die better
Than by facing fearful odds
For the ashes of his fathers,
For the temples of his gods?

In the midst of all these scams, scandals and squabbles we need to remember that.

■■

ALIENS IN OWN LAND

At the time of Partition, quite a few Sikh and some Hindu families from Peshawar moved over to Kabul and other places in Afghanistan. They had their relatives there. Settled in Afghanistan for a long period, most of these relatives were engaged in dry fruit and cloth business.

There were others too, like them, who had their roots in the tribal areas of the NWFP. They were called Terais. When communal trouble spread over the tribal areas, these people descended on Peshawar. They, too, were rich and purchased a large number of houses in the city. Later, in 1947, many of them migrated to Afghanistan.

There was money in Afghanistan. It was commonly said in Peshawar that cloth worth Rs 10,000 in the city could easily fetch over a lakh in Kabul. The *tehsildar* of Landikotal, the last railway station on the North-Western Railway, was known to be fabulously wealthy. No truck could pass through his territory, this way or that, without his permission.

The Terais and the Afghanis of Indian origin were, in several respects, like the rest of us in Peshawar – raw, ready to shoot, uncivilised (from today's standards). They wore the same type of clothes, the same type of turbans, and spoke the same language as we did – Hindko, a mixture of Punjabi and Pushtu, with a sprinkling of Persian.

They were all uneducated but deeply religious. They won't touch *halal* meat. And since *jhattka* meat was not easily available in Peshawar, they used to buy sheep and slaughter them in the *jhattka* way at home. A sheep a day was the norm of an average family. In my locality, *mohalla* Kakaran, we used to see fresh blood of sheep coming down the drain-pipes of Terai houses almost every morning.

We used to envy them. They had 303 rifles whereas we had only 12-bore double-barrel guns. They would flourish their revolvers as against our pistols at common meetings held to consider how best to protect the locality against gangs of communal marauders from outside. Of course, many of these weapons were indigenously made which was evident from the "Made in Ingland" mark that these generally carried.

Today's Afghanistan is different. Every eighth person is maimed. That is the price of a long civil war. All the Terais and other Afghans of Indian origin living in that country must pack up and go. Some of them are already in India.

But what has made them do so. Why have they deserted the land of their forefathers? Because they are sinners? Sinners? Yes, their religion is different from the ones they shared their happiness and sorrow with! And that too for decades, if not centuries.

The 20th century is coming to an end. We are an advanced civilisation, we say. What an advancement!

■■

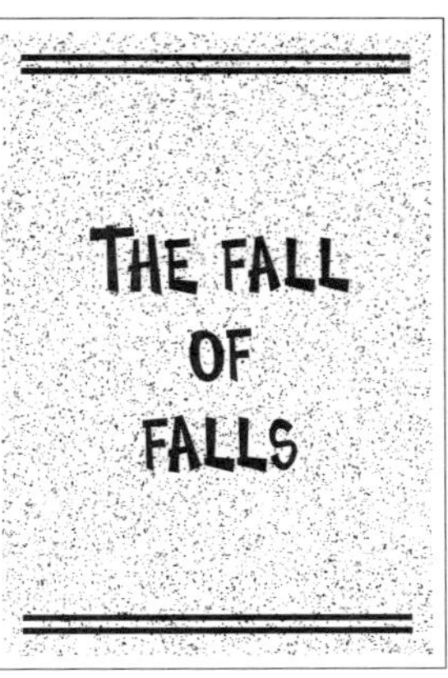

Not all of us can afford to go to a hill station during summer. And not all those who go can afford to stay in a hotel. In Shimla, a room alone in a modest hotel on The Mall costs Rs 500 a day. Ten days' stay in the town can mean over Rs 10,000! Who can afford it? Certainly not those in the fixed income group.

But even though man has become increasingly self-centred, mercifully, we in India continue to cherish the values of those invisibly tender bonds that bind kith and kin together. When we visit some city other than our own and know that there is a relative or some old friend residing there, we, at least the old-fashioned amongst us, prefer to stay with him or her. And he, too, welcomes us. It is a reciprocal arrangement, though now on the wane.

My wife and I are lucky that every summer we are able to spend a few weeks in Shimla; our elder daughter and son-in-law live there. They have a guest room in their house. We stay in this and they take all pains to ensure our comfort so much so that sometimes we feel embarrassed by what they do for us.

Frankly, I am in love with the Shimla Hills. In my young days, I used to roam about on the mountains, and there is hardly a place in the region which I have not gone to. It used to be such a great pleasure to climb up to the Jakhu Hill top or amble down to the Glen, or walk through the half-a-mile long Barogh tunnel.

At 70, I cannot do that kind of thing. But out of curiosity, I asked an old friend about the Chadwick Falls. I asked him about the Falls, because while I had heard people talking about going to Mushobra, Kufri, Chail, Wildflower Hall, and multitudinous other places, I had heard none mentioning the Chadwick Falls. Way back in the 40s, I had experienced the exhilarating thrill of the splash of their chilly water on my bare body.

"Chadwick Falls?" My friend was taken aback and added laughing heartily, "those dried up long years ago. Shimla now has only three kinds of falls – snowfall, rainfall and 'guestfall'(!). Right now it is the season of 'guestfall'. There is no other fall anywhere around."

Apparently, like most other permanent residents of Shimla, he had more guests at his place than he could possibly cope with. I felt small.

■■

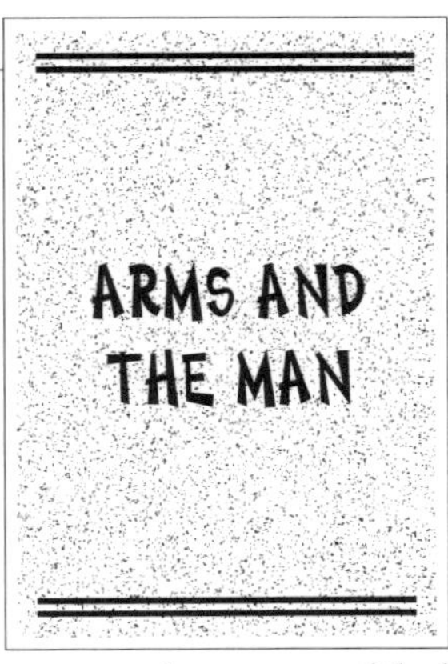

Arms and the Man

Laloo and his clan in Bihar have their lathis. Togadia in Rajasthan and the likes of him in Gujarat are brandishing their trishuls. Thakur Amar Singh has taken out his sword to behead anyone who dares tangle with him. And so it goes, this search for private weaponry.

Men with fading memories – such as yours truly – are entitled to ask where all this will lead to ultimately. Will the battle of Kurukshetra, they all seem to be fighting, solve any of the problems the country is facing today?

Involuntarily, I am carried back to the days of my youth. Yes, it was the month of March in 1947 and it was in Peshawar. Communal riots were at their peak. I was a post-graduate student in the Islamia College. Like the rest of the non-Muslim students in the college, I was expelled from the hostel. Tribal lords on the Hindukush mountains had threatened to invade the college since it had given shelter to non-Muslim students, and the principal thought it prudent to get rid of us – some forty students, out of a thousand or so.

We were virtually imprisoned in our non-Muslim mohallas. How were we to defend these mohallas? How were we to protect our mothers and sisters? Meetings were held every evening to evolve strategies.

Some Sikhs from the tribal area, known as Tarais, ousted from their homes, had also come to live in our mohalla. They were rich people and had purchased houses there. I don't know for sure where they got their money from but it was commonly believed that – like the Afghan tribals – they were deeply involved in the illicit trade in hashish and the like.

Every evening, security duties were assigned to the young men in mohalla to protect it at night in the event of an attack. These duties were assigned, keeping in view the nature of the threat and the weapons we possessed. My father had purchased for me a Webster pistol and I had a retainer's licence for it.

At one meeting held to discuss the rnohalla's defence, everybody was asked to display the weapon he possessed. When my turn came, I took out my Webster pistol with great pride and held it aloft.

"This kind of toy," said Bhai Jaimal Singh, one of the richest tribals from the mountains who had landed in our mohalla, and who had with him a .303 rifle, gifted to him, or so he claimed, by the king of Afghanistan, "our women keep with them. They play with them. Better put it back in your pocket."

Needless to say, my little pistol was destroyed in the holocaust that followed and which resulted in India's partition. It had been of little use.

■■

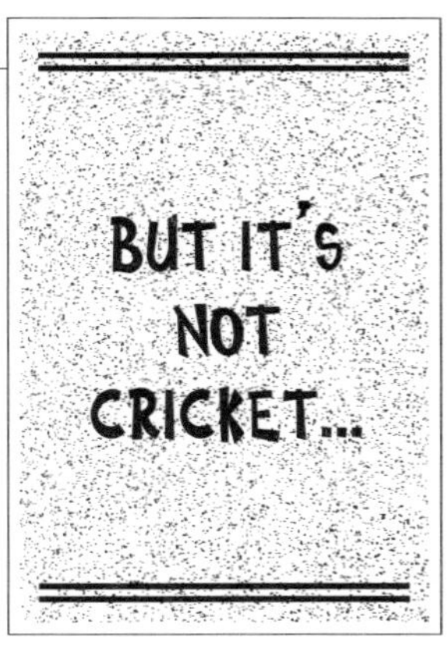

I was watching the cricket match between India and Pakistan in Chennai on TV and Peshawar suddenly appeared before my eyes. My mind played the same trick a second time when I watched the match between the two teams in Delhi, again on TV. Which team belongs where? Which is the one from Pakistan? Which from India? Could anyone watching the crowd cheering the Pakistani team at Chennai say that that team was from Pakistan, and not from India?

March 10, 1947 – we received verbal orders from the Principal of the Islamia College, Peshawar, to vacate our hostel the same day. The next day, March 11, the NFWP Assembly was to meet. The Congress Party under Dr Khan Sahib was in power. The Muslim League had declared that it would not allow the Assembly to meet. According to our Principal, the tribals living in villages around had threatened that they would make mincemeat of all Hindu and Sikh students the same day. We had to leave. And we left. How many were wounded? How many lost their belongings? That is not the picture my mind conjured up as I watched those cricket hatches.

Two weeks of incarceration in my own *mohalla*, along with all the others, arrival of the wounded from here and there, visit to Pancteerath – the cremation ground – to identify bodies of people who were no more, day and night vigil within the locality to see that none from outside infiltrated there – no, not all this.

Again the mind's images as I watched the two cricket matches were not this.

Rather, it was an altogether different spectacle. Something, I am more familiar with and which recurs ever so often. I am sitting atop the *mohalla pati* (iron gate). It is late in the night. I have a pistol in my hand. What is its range? How far could a bullet go? I don't remember. What I remember is the sound of footsteps. As they came closer and others at the gate along with me heard it and grew tense, we discovered that it was Dr Khan Sahib, the Premier himself, along with a large posse of armed police, who had come to our rescue. We opened the gate.

The entire *mohalla* collected around him. He had words of solace for all. And true to his word, he helped us move out the next day. Lines of red shirts (Khudai Khidmatgaars) were there on both sides of the road to protect us.

This is the image that lingers on. And then I find myself on the lawns of the Rashtrapati Bhavan in Delhi. Dr Khan is there at the invitation of Jawaharlal. I am heading the Republic Day troupe from UP. I request him to pose with us for a group photograph. He does. Does he remember who I am? I don't know. Jawaharlal is with him.

We pine for what is not; our sweetest songs are those that tell us of the saddest thought. Will the cricket matches that India and Pakistan played fall into that category?

I hope not.

Will they usher in a new era? I hope so.

■■

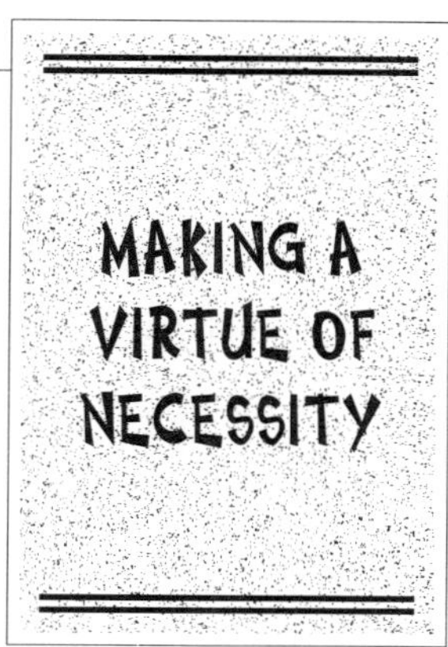

A renowned Hollywood actress, living in virtual retirement, basking in the glory of her magnificent past, had a pleasant surprise one evening. Two gentlemen, a producer and a director, both upcoming and on the road to fame, called on her. She had known them and was delighted to receive them.

They talked about her great past and then came to brasstacks and narrated to her the script of a new film which they wanted to make. The story ran like this: An ambitious American millionaire and his equally ambitious wife, chase money all the time in order to lead a good life; they succeed in their pursuit, but since they have the same likes and dislikes, they get fed up with each other and separate; the man marries and divorces half a dozen other women; the woman, too, marries and divorces half a dozen other men; eventually they meet again, remarry, discover the meaning of good life, give up chasing money and live happily thereafter.

The actress was fascinated and asked excitedly, "What is going to be my role in this?" The gentlemen were greatly embarrassed. For, they had not come to offer her a role in the film. One of the scenes in it was to depict what good life used to be earlier in the century. This required an ancient car of a certain make and that was not available with anyone except the renowned actress. They wanted this car on loan from her. The lady understood the situation, smiled and agreed to lend them the car with the clear understanding that they would handle it lovingly as a baby.

I had read the story in some American magazine many years ago. It came back to me like a flash on a Sunday afternoon in December when an old colleague, whom I had not seen for almost a decade, suddenly descended on us along with his wife.

We exchanged the customary pleasantries, my wife prepared coffee and we talked about what we had done or failed to do since we had met last. This done, I inquisitively asked him what it was that had brought him to my place. "Shall I tell you the truth?" he asked, somewhat hesitatingly.

"Of course," I answered, "tell me if there is anything I can do for you. It will be my pleasure."

"Nothing of the sort," he quipped, "it is just that there is hardly any occasion to use the car these days. And if it is not used, the battery goes down. To prevent that, I have to drive the blessed thing some distance at least once a week. Today, we thought we might call on you. Killing two birds with one stone, you see."

■■

CLOUDS OVER KHYBER PASS

As usual, Haddow Harris was having his evening class on the road to Khyber Pass, just outside the sprawling Islamia College campus, seven miles north of Peshawar and some twenty miles this side of Landikotal, the last town on the Indo-Afghan border. In those days, in 1946, it was dangerous to move about on that road in the evening. But Harris, who was the Head of the Department of English in our college, was a Scotsman. He was sure that nobody would touch him.

Our class (M.A. in English) consisted of only three students – Habib, Haq and I. The way of teaching that Harris followed was as unique as was our college. A bit of textbook work in the classroom in the morning, a bit more of it over tea at his residence (it was a residential institution) and detailed elaboration later on the road to Khyber Pass – it was altogether different from the mushroom-type education in vogue today.

The college was unique in the sense that throughout our stay there we never saw the face of a woman. The British teachers preferred to live alone. Wives and daughters of Muslim dons did come out in the evening but they always wore long *burqas*, down to their ankles, and had armed guards as their shadows.

Another unique thing about the college was that for eleven years nobody had passed his M.A. in English from it. Harris used to tell us that the Punjab University would abolish the class if nobody got through in the 1947 examination also.

"I would be happy to go back to Scotland," he would add, "but it will be my eternal regret that I could not turn out one single M.A. from this blessed college."

Naturally he bestowed all his attention on us. That evening the sky was overcast. Harris looked at the clouds and recited three poems – English, Latin, Greek – in their praise. Then he looked at Habib and asked him, "what do you think?"

Habib was puzzled. He, too, looked at the clouds, then at us, and blurted out, "Sir, it looks as if it is going to rain."

"You bloody Pathans," Harris roared, "you will never be able to appreciate poetry. It demands concentration. But you cannot sit in a chair for more than half an hour. Your fingers start itching for the gun."

There was no rain on the Khyber Pass that evening. Nor was there any examination in 1947. Lahore was our centre. It was in turmoil. So was Peshawar. Haq was from the Punjab and, therefore, an alien in those parts. He ran away conveniently. Habib retreated to his village near Peshawar. I had to come over to India and passed the examination which the Punjab University finally held in Delhi in 1948.

But Harris did not leave the college because of us. Indeed he left before the riots and for an altogether different reason.

He had to go to the radio station in Peshawar. The tongas were on strike. Someone succeeded in arranging one for him. The strikers waylaid the tonga. They did no harm to Harris. Nor to the tonga driver. But they stabbed the mare.

That was too much for the sensitive mind of Harris. He just could not bear the sight, packed up and left for home leaving behind his best wishes for the three of us.

■■

VIEW FROM SHIMLA

"Look" I pleaded with the police official, "I have come after a long walk and I am feeling somewhat tired. I am leaning on this railing just for a little respite. I have no intention to stick on to it."

The cop was adamant, but polite. "You are," he said, "twice my age. But if I allow you to stay on here, more people will come and then it may become difficult. The instructions to me are that I should keep the railing clear."

It was about eleven in the morning in Shimla. The President of India was in town. He was to come from one side of the Mall and to move on to the other. The police had used a long rope to cut the road into two parts, the smaller one, some four feet wide, for the people to walk through, and the larger one, twenty or more feet wide, for the smooth passage of the President's caravan.

The railing is on the other side of the Scandal Point from where one can look down on the Mall. The police had their reasons to guard it. I did not want to argue with the cop but what I had witnessed earlier in the course of my walk from the Ridge to the Legislative Assembly building and back had made me immensely sad and I felt like protesting.

All along the route, I had seen policemen asking the people to keep on moving on their part of the road. At one spot, a horse appeared from somewhere. "Take it away," shouted an officer. At another, a coolie, carrying three or four suitcases on his back, stopped for a while, placed the suitcases on a small side wall and sat down, apparently to recoup his strength. He was made to go down the hill, along with the suitcases.

"At what time is the President coming?" I asked the cop at the railing.

"Anytime now," he replied, "but I cannot say. I do not know."

"Since when have you been on duty here?"

"Since early in the morning," he said, and added quickly, straightening the white V.V.I. P. Duty Slip pinned awkwardly on his chest, "kindly move away, my officer is coming."

Every visit of the President adds to the importance of Shimla. It also perhaps helps the State Government in moving towards the realisation of its proclaimed goal of converting Himachal into another Switzerland on God's little earth.

And I realise that in these days of high risk to high dignitaries, with whom is linked the future of India, security measures are an inevitable necessity. But as I left the railing and walked to the residence of Harsh and Renu, my children, a long-lost gem of wisdom from Sarojini Naidu sparkled in my mind.

She was supervising the arrangements that were being made for the stay of Mahatma Gandhi in the Bhangi Colony in Delhi in 1947 or so. She paused for a while, looked around, took a deep breath and then whispered, "if only the Mahatma knew how much it costs us to make life simple for him!"

■■

PUT IN PLACE

"I want to go to El Dorado," said the Minister to his Private Secretary, "get in touch with our embassy there and their embassy here. The ideal time will be when the Prime Minister is abroad."

"I will contact the two embassies immediately, Sir," the PS replied, mighty pleased that he too would get the opportunity to tag along on the junket.

"But, Sir," he asked the Minister, after a pause, "what do I tell the two embassies? I mean, in order to be prepared duly they will have to draw up a befitting schedule for you."

"That," the Minister dismissed him sternly, "you better settle with the officer concerned. Let me see the programme by Monday."

"Yes, Sir," said the PS.

Back in his room, the PS scratched his head and decided that the only person who could help in the matter was the Under Secretary in charge of the foreign desk. The issue being sensitive, naturally he first thought of the Joint Secretary, two steps above the US, but he had to drop the idea because a proposal for the Jt. Secy.'s own month-long tour of China had been turned down only a day earlier by the Minister on the ground that too many officers were visiting China without India gaining anything.

He had also thought of taking advice from the wise old Deputy Secretary. But then he knew that the Dy. Secy. was in an awfully hostile mood. He had risen from the ranks and was due for promotion to the post of Jt. Secy. but suddenly a young IAS officer had descended on the scene and pushed him aside. The PS decided not to bother him.

As he walked into the room of the US, the latter felt highly honoured and rose in his seat. 'Official coffee', which means special coffee for special occasions at State expense, was ordered immediately. "I know El Dorado," the US pronounced with absolute confidence, "there will be no problem in drawing up a programme."

The two of them jointly tried to locate El Dorado on the map of the world. They could not locate it. The Section Officer was called. He, too, could not locate it. The assistant who processes foreign visit cases was tapped discreetly. He had not heard of the place.

Finally, the US rang up his counterpart in the External Affairs Ministry, whom he knew intimately.

The latter laughed heartily and asked him to look up the dictionary.

"Why dictionary?" said the US, I have done a thorough scanning of the map."

"See the dictionary also," the EA man insisted.

The dictionary was seen. The two gentlemen were flabbergasted to find in it that El Dorado meant "a fictitious country or city abounding in gold."

Timidly, the PS walked into the Minister's room and told him what was what. The Minister flew into a rage. "Dirty fellows, dirty tricks," he railed, showering imprecations on God knows whom.

"Who gave you the proposal, Sir?" asked the PS.

"Leave me alone," bemoaned the Minister.

■■

My friend, Gugga, ran away from the King Edwards College, Peshawar, in the mid-forties and joined the Indian Army. Not that he had any special liking for the Army. He was a jolly good fellow, fond of telling juicy tales, and was as popular with men as with women.

He would have preferred to join his family's flourishing cloth business in the city. But then his father, a widower, himself married the girl he had chosen for Gugga. That was not uncommon in Peshawar. Men were terribly manly in that town.

Anyhow Gugga ran away from home and became a VCO (Viceroy's Commissioned Officer) in the Royal Indian Army Service Corps (RIASC). There he was given a fascinating job – to censor letters that were exchanged between soldiers on the war front and their families back home.

Whenever he used to come to Peshawar on furlough, he would narrate to us in the Sarbdayal Garden countless stories of romance – men's hunger for their wives and warm responses from the latter, as revealed in their intimate letters.

Gugga was demobbed at the end of the war. After Partition, he tried hard to settle down in Delhi. He would buy neckties and hankies in Chandni Chowk and sell them at higher rates in Connaught Place. This went on for a while till he spotted a good-looking girl from a well-to-do family. Handsome and jovial as Gugga was, the girl fell in love with him almost at first sight. Gugga married her promptly.

The girl's father was a big hide and skin merchant. He asked Gugga to set up a branch of his firm in Amritsar. Gugga did not like the smell of hides and skins but then his wife, apparently with an eye on the future, egged him on and Gugga surrendered. In course of time, he became proprietor of the firm he established in Amritsar.

Till Punjab was lost to insanity by the troubles of the eighties, I used to visit Gugga in Amritsar off and on. There he would take me to the hide market. Villagers, mostly Sikhs, brought skins of goats and sheep to the market and these were auctioned.

The auction system, called parchi (chit), was peculiar. Skins were sold not in lots, but one by one. The bids were written on small chits of paper. Whosoever's chit quoted the highest price for a skin displayed, the skin was given to him. The process lasted a few minutes, depending on the number of skins sold.

Each skin bore a name, given to it by the villager who brought it or by the merchants assembled at the auction. The name was always that of a well-known political leader of the day. If 20 skins were sold at a particular auction, that could mean, amusingly or shockingly, according to one's susceptibilities, sale (probably hawala, whatever that means) of 20 political leaders in the hide market of Amritsar on that occasion!

Both the villagers and merchants were very fair. Names of large size leaders were bestowed on large size skins. Similarly, small size skins bore the names of leaders with meagre dimensions. Their colour and sex were always taken into account. Caste and community did not matter.

When things became somewhat hot in Amritsar, Gugga toyed with the idea of shifting his business to Delhi. He had to give it up for he did not find it feasible.

"How are things now?" I asked him when he came to my place early in November this year, while on a visit to the Capital.

"Fine," he said, "the only difference is that Akali leaders are more popular these days. Villagers like to give their names to the skins of goats and sheep they bring. Earlier this privilege belonged almost exclusively to Congress leaders."

■■

How was my speech in Parliament?" asked the minister, floating in the air.

"Excellent," said the secretary.

"More than excellent," added the additional secretary, mindful of his position in the official hierarchy and refusing to be one of those who also serve who only stand and wait.

"Normally I do not open my mouth in Parliament," the minister mused. "How many people are there? You can count them on your fingers. I am not used to addressing small gatherings. I have made speeches at meetings attended by lakhs.

"To speak to the masses has its own charm. It exhilarates you. It excites you. It gives you new ideas. It gives you new enthusiasm. Every time I address a large gathering, I feel so young. I feel like Rani *ki* Jhansi."

"Rani *ki* Jhansi, Sir?" Intervened the secretary.

"No, Jhansi *ki* Rani," said the minister, "slip of the tongue."

"But she was a woman," submitted the additional secretary respectfully.

"Yes, she was a woman," remarked the minister somewhat loudly, "but she represented more than what a woman can represent. She represented the glory of India, the greatness of India, the peaks of its mountains, the courage of its people, the bravery of its soldiers, the manhood of its men. I feel like Jhansi *ki* Rani. I feel like Tantia Topi.

"I am used to multitudes. Not to hundreds. Half the members do not come to Parliament at all. Out of those who come, half mark themselves present in the morning and then disappear. The quorum bell is ringing all the time. How can you unburden yourself to empty benches?"

"But you spoke very well, Sir," said the secretary.

"That is because," said the minister, inflating his chest and rolling up the loose sleeves of his shirt, "I had to speak. So many ideas had accumulated within me. They had reached their boiling point. If I had not brought them out today, they would have burst my chest and throttled my throat."

"You presented them in a very cogent manner, Sir," said the secretary.

"Your speeches, Sir," butted in the additional secretary, "are no ordinary speeches. They are thoughts collected in tranquillity – dissertations on the subjects you touch."

"Yes," warmed up the minister, "I will dissect anyone who tries to intervene when I am on my feet. I am all for maintaining decorum in Parliament and for freedom of speech. But that does not mean that I will allow anyone to deny me my own right to freedom of speech."

"You are absolutely right," said the secretary, looking first at his deputy who, he felt, was trying to outsmart him by talking philosophy, and then at the minister. "And if I may say so," he said, "you spoke like Cicero."

"Who was Cicero?" asked the minister.

Before either of the two gentlemen could answer the question, an aide appeared on the scene and whispered something into the ear of the minister who moved away with him.

After he had gone, the additional secretary looked at his boss and inquired, "What speech was he referring to?"

"I do not know," answered the boss.

"Then how did you say it was excellent?" asked the additional secretary.

"Just as you said that it was more than excellent," replied the secretary.

■■

Ram Bharose is an experienced MLA, master in the art of jumping from one party to another. On him depended the fate of the government. It happened like this. There was a no-confidence motion in the Legislative Assembly against the government. The hotch-potch collage that constituted it had the same strength as the hotch-potch collage that was the Opposition. Both were equally divided. The views of the Speaker, who was supposed to be above all parties, were not known. He had served the two largest parties on both sides with equal distinction.

If only one MLA from the Opposition could abstain from the vote, the government could survive. Ram Bharose's name came to everyone's lips. He could be persuaded not to attend the Assembly on the crucial day. A delegation of three important leaders of the ruling hotch-potch, known for their persuasive abilities, was deputed to meet Ram Bharose.

Ram Bharose was not an easy nut to crack. He was willing and yet not willing. He said that even though as a matter of principle, he would stand by the opposition, he could change his mind and abstain if he could be appointed a member of the cabinet after the government won the vote of confidence. That was not acceptable. Nine out of every ten members of the coalition were already ministers.

A good deal of bargaining was done. Finally it was agreed that Ram Bharose should constitute a one-man goodwill delegation from India to some foreign land. Which foreign land? UK? No, Ram Bharose had already been there several times. France? No, he did not know the French language. Germany? No, what will

Ram Bharose do there? Nobody would recognise him as a great Indian leader in Germany. US? That is where the action is. Ram Bharose agreed. Then the question arose: what will Ram Bharose's one-man goodwill delegation do in the US? It will build bridges of understanding between India and the US.

That done, Ram Bharose developed chest pain and was airlifted to New Delhi and promptly admitted in the All India Institute of Medical Sciences. A team of doctors examined him and declared his condition stable. The team said that Ram Bharose should be kept under observation for some days. Meanwhile, the crucial no-confidence motion came up in the Assembly. The government survived the vote of no-confidence. And true to the best traditions of Indian democracy, it stood by its promise to Ram Bharose and sent him to the US immediately on discharge from AIIMS.

What did Ram Bharose do in the US? Nobody knows for sure. The last I heard was that he was attending a conference of the world's top religious leaders on transcendental meditation in California as India's distinguished one-man delegation.

■■

Welcome once again to Kaun Banega Pradhan Mantri. You saw last night how Har Fun Maula walked away from here as a minister in the Union cabinet. Tonight, we have 10 new contestants. Give them a big hand. As usual, we will play the fastest finger first. You know the rules.

Four names will appear on your computer screen. You have to arrange them according to their age, from the youngest to the oldest. Whosoever does it first will sit with me on that seat over there. Narasimha Rao, Sonia Gandhi, Jyoti Basu, Arjun Singh. The correct answer is Sonia Gandhi, Arjun Singh, Narasimha Rao, Jyoti Basu. Only three of you have hit the nail on the head. But Ajoy Bagchi from Calcutta has done it first. Best of luck to Ajoyji.

Your first question, Ajoyji. At Sangam in Allahabad, three rivers meet – Ganga, Yamuna and a third one that is invisible. Which is this – Ravi, Godavari, Saraswati, Narbada? Saraswati. Sure? Yes, sure. Shall we lock it? Yes. Correct.

Your second question. Who was the heroine of Chhamian? Madhuri Dixit, Hema Malini, Begam Para, Nurjahan? Begam Para. Sure? Computerji, lock Begam Para. Correct.

Your third question. Which of the prime ministers of India never faced Parliament? Morarji Desai, Charan Singh, Lal Bahadur Shastri, Rajiv Gandhi? Charan Singh. Sure? Sure. Shall I lock it? Lock him. Correct. That, too, is correct.

Your fourth question, Ajoyji. Which Indian minister died of a fast unto death? Gulzari Lal Nanda, Raj Narain, Jagjivan Ram, none? None? That, too, is correct. And with it, you have crossed the first milestone. That means you have become an MP. That also means whatever else happens, you go from here as an MP.

Now the track is a bit uphill. If you cross it, you become a full-blown minister. Your first question. How many free calls can an MP make from his telephones in a year? 25,000; 50,000; one lakh; 1.5 lakh. Doubt in your mind? You can use any of your three lifelines: phone a friend, audience poll, fifty-fifty. What? You want to phone Laloo Yadav? Computerji, connect Lalooji. What does he say? Limitless. For Lalooji, everything is limitless. You want to use another lifeline? Yes, audience poll. Eighty per cent say 1.5 lakh. I will go with the audience. Correct. Thanks to the audience. You have become a minister.

Your next question now is: "That shows how dangerous it is to be too good". On the assassination of Mahatma Gandhi, who made that famous statement? Jawaharlal Nehru, Bernard Russell, Dr Radhakrishnan, George Bernard Shaw? Correct answer to that will make you India's Pradhan Mantri. Pause. Long pause. I will go in for fifty-fifty. Computerji, remove the two wrong answers. Removed. The choice now is between Nehru and GBS. Pause again. Nehru. Sure? Sure. Lock him? Yes. Sorry, Ajoyji, that is wrong. It was George Bernard Shaw.

Never mind. Better luck next time. But tell me, if you had become Pradhan Mantri, what would have been your first act?

I would have appointed you as my finance minister and Veerappan as my home minister.

■■

It was only a meeting of fingers. Cool, condescending, almost unwilling. The wrist was not involved. Nor the rest of the hand. Fingers, too, just the two of them, the index and the middle one. Not the thumb, not the last two. The same was not the behaviour of my hand. It had stretched forth, obediently. Not that warmly, I concede. But apprehensively. Afraid of being rejected? I won't know.

That was not the case, much later, in May 1964, when I saw a swarm of fingers clutching the bars of the Teen Murti House in New Delhi. I didn't see those fingers in flesh and bones. I saw them only in a photograph which T Kasinath or maybe someone else had captured with his camera. The fingers reflected the agony; the anguish, the helplessness of those to whom these belonged. Multitudes. Wanting to gatecrash into that house. To go there and to have a last glimpse of their beloved leader, Jawaharlal Nehru. His body lay inside, being readied to be taken out on its last journey. Jawaharlal was no more. Suddenly a vacuum occurred in countless hearts. How could fingers fill that vacuum? When I first used that photograph in an exhibition in Rabindra Bhavan, all traffic stopped. No, there were no tears in any eyes. Tears have a limited life. Voids, too, do not remain voids for long. Their memory lasts.

Returning to those cool and condescending fingers, it was just a little before India was partitioned and I was thrown out of my hometown, Peshawar. I wish Karsh of Ottawa was there to capture them. In many a photograph that he took, including that of Jawaharlal, fingers, furrows and lines come out prominently to tell what goes on inside their owner's mind. What was going on in my mind? What was going on in the mind of the man to whom those cool and condescending fingers belonged? Karsh of Ottawa was not there to tell that tale. The nearest I can come to it is Oscar Wilde. He was being taken to prison for a crime he had not committed. There was no one to tell him that he had done no wrong. No one to say goodbye to him. Then, a sentry at the prison gate touched his hat. Oscar Wilde recalls the poignancy of that moment in his *De Profundis*.

My moment was altogether different. Locale – my alma mater, Islamia College. Occasion – function in honour of M A Jinnah. The touch and go fingers belonged to him.

■■

When I took on rent the upper portion of his house in Patel Nagar in the sixties, it did not occur to me that he belonged to a different community. I knew that he was a Sikh and I a Hindu. But this was like two persons bearing two different names. I believe at that time he, too, did not have any antipathy to Hindus. He would not have taken me as a tenant otherwise.

He himself lived on the ground floor. His family was large. Still he had rented two of the four rooms with him to another family. This happened after I had moved in. I could do nothing about it, though it did affect adversely the water supply to my portion of the house.

Gradually the man revealed himself. He had all the traits of a cunning, greedy landlord. He had told me verbally that the terrace on the top was an integral part of the upper portion and the rent was inclusive of it. He denied me its use on the pretext that he had plans to construct a *barsati* on it. The main electricity and water switches were on the ground floor. He would put them off frequently.

During the five years that I stayed in that house, he increased the rent heavily twice. I had to yield. The third demand was made on religious grounds. The man said that he was a religious person and as a matter of policy, he had decided to give his house on rent to Sikhs only.

This demand was followed by a threatening letter from a gentleman whom I did not know but who claimed to be the office-bearer of some fifteen societies, mostly Sikh, in West Delhi. He directed me to meet him at once in my own interest. I did not meet him but left the house. I was already looking for another.

Time has blurred the pages of that bad chapter from the book of my life. But another chapter remains.

It relates to the man's mother.

Seventy or so, the old lady was treated worse than a maid-servant. Early in the morning, she was sent to the milk-booth to fetch milk. Then began the endless ritual of cooking, cleaning utensils, cleaning the house, which included lavatory, and making paper-bags which the family sold to shopkeepers. Almost every day the man's wife, who had grown-up sons and daughters, used to beat her. "When will the Lord release me from this body?" The old lady used to cry.

But for some reasons, the Lord did not oblige her. At night, when the man returned home from his work, his wife would invariably flare up at him. "Your mother," she would shout, "has made life miserable for me. Either she lives in this house or I."

She was given to hysteria. Faked or genuine, I cannot say. Sometimes, she would run out of the house. The man would follow her and bring her back. We often heard him telling her, "don't you worry. Old women generally die in winter."

Opposite that house, across the road, used to live a noble lady, Mrs Bakhshi. Her son, Ashok, and my son, Prem, were close friends. They continue to be so. Recently when Ashok returned from England, where he was a Punjab National Bank executive, there was a get-together in his house. I, too, went there.

"How is the old lady?" I asked Ashok.

"God listened to her prayers, after all," said Ashok, "and she cleared whatever debts she might have owed to them in some previous life. She died the day Mrs Gandhi was assassinated.

"That day, hooligans attacked a number of Sikh houses in the locality. They came to her son's house also. They saw her body lying in the verandah outside, bowed before it and went away."

■■

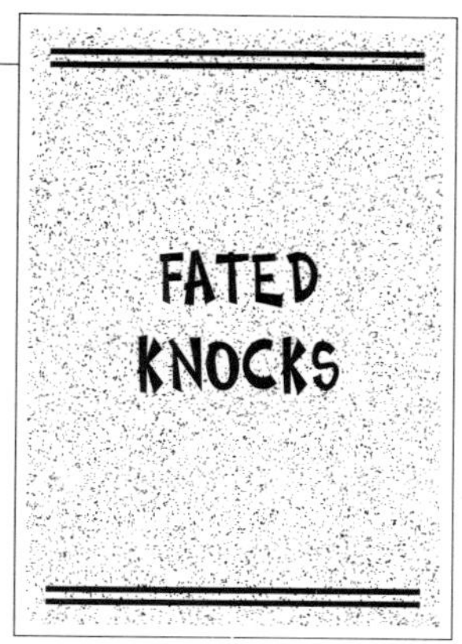

He was apparently not over-speeding. But his motor-cycle was on the right-hand side of the road. I was coming from the opposite direction, blew the horn, slowed my car and eventually stopped it.

The Sardarji realised his mistake rather late. Quickly he tried to swerve to the left but could not avoid the accident. The two-wheeler banged into the car and crashed on the road along with the rider.

I came out and helped the man in getting up. He was injured and obviously in pain. "Please forgive me," he muttered, "I was lost in my own tangles."

There was blood on his trousers and sleeves of his shirt. Both were torn. He looked at himself, wiped off the dust from his hands and added, "God has saved me, only minor injuries. But please do take me to the hospital. The fault was entirely mine. Nothing will happen to you."

The motor-cycle was badly damaged. One of the headlights of the car was also smashed. The man, obviously above fifty, pushed the motor-cycle to the edge of the road and pleaded with me again, "please do take me to the hospital. I assure you nothing will happen to you."

For a split second, the thought of the meeting I was to attend at the India International Centre on the same road crossed my mind. But it vanished as it came.

"How did it happen?" I asked him on the way to the Lohia Hospital.

"Whatever God ordains," he answered philosophically, "has to happen. Who can escape it? Pakistan, then these Delhi riots;

could we prevent either? The Lord willed it that way. So did He will this accident."

It was just about a year after the assassination of Mrs Indira Gandhi. In the casualty ward of the hospital, the doctor on duty heard the word accident and pronounced promptly "lego-medical case". Two police constables, seemingly on perpetual duty there, rushed to the scene almost menacingly and got ready to record the victim's statement on loose sheets of paper held together by an archaic metallic device on an archaic wooden plank.

Their very sight disturbed me. Was I in for some trouble? That fear did come but then I gathered myself and asked the doctor, "please attend to his injuries first."

As he started doing so, the Sardarji looked at me, then at the two constables, and said, "there is nothing for you, brothers. I was going on my motor-cycle. It fell down. This gentleman saw me. He has brought me here. May God bless him."

Outside, as he was buying medicines prescribed by the doctor from the chemist's shop, I asked him, "what happens to your motorcycle?"

"I will send my son to pick it up," he replied.

"May I drop you home?" I suggested.

"Which side do you live?" he asked.

"Tara Apartments in South Delhi," I answered.

"Then no, sir," he folded his hands, "I live far away, near Gandhi Nagar. I am all right. I will go somehow. But will you do me another favour?"

As I looked at him inquisitively, he added, "kindly leave your address with me. I will send my son to your place to pay for the damages I have caused to your car."

■■

KHANS OF KASHMIR

As the bus from Delhi reached the bus-stand on the Cart Road in Shimla, there was a pell-mell. The passengers inside were exhausted. They wanted to get out quickly. Outside, the porters had virtually blocked the door.

"Sahib, take my number," they shouted, the frantic entreaties betraying a note of desperation. The numbers, inscribed on small metallic plates, were the licences that permitted them to work as porters in the town. Each one of them tried to pass on his number to one passenger or another. The moment he succeeded in doing so, he felt relieved, like someone who had made advance payment for something which was in short supply.

The more the number of suitcases, the happier the porter. He does not want to share his load with any other porter. For that would mean sharing of the earning as well. Up the hill he goes, unmindful of his bent back, faster than you can follow him. He reaches your hotel before you can make up to it. And he delivers your luggage to you intact. Nothing opened. Nothing missing. Only the leather suit-cases bear the marks of his strong rope. Like the marks on his own body.

Strangely, I found a remarkable camaraderie among the porters, Himachalis and Kashmiris. At the bus-stand their features distinguished them, though not very clearly. Somebody said that this year, there was a greater influx of porters from Kashmir. I asked the one who brought my luggage to where I stayed. "Yes," he said, "from my district, Anantnang alone, we are more than 2,000. We come here every year as the season starts and go back before Id."

"Where do you live here?" I asked.

"In mosques and *deras*," he replied, "we go there only to sleep and to offer *namaz*. Otherwise, the whole day we are busy. So many buses come and go. This year, by the grace of God, there is greater tourist traffic here. Nobody goes to Kashmir. There *amman* (peace) has been destroyed."

I could not resist the temptation to ask him about Pakistan. "Yes," he said, "many go there, too. Mostly young people, having no jobs. There they are given money and *aslah* (weapons). To attack their own *mulak* (country). Our need brings us here. Their compulsion takes them there. Once they get caught in the net, only death can disentangle them. The reality is that there is no one to give them correct guidance. All our leaders have run away from Kashmir. And God alone knows what has happened to all the money that people say Delhi has been sending to Kashmir for ages."

The man was quite volatile. He was not educated and that made mockery of the claim that education in Kashmir is free up to the University level. Around forty, he had obviously been a part of the tragedy that Kashmir is today.

"Have others from your village also gone to Pakistan for the kind of work you do in Shimla?" I asked him hesitatingly.

"Yes," he replied promptly and clearly, "but most of them have come back."

"Why?" I queried.

He smiled and said sarcastically, "They call them *Hato* there. You know what *Hato* means? It is a word full of contempt, used for those inferior to you. The British called us *Hato* as they called you *Kala admi*."

"What do they call you here in Shimla?" I asked.

He smiled, paused and then said somewhat philosophically: "Well, here in Shimla, here they call us Khan. *Achha lagta hae* (it sounds good). If all one's life one has to carry others' load, it is better to carry it as a Khan than as a *Hato*."

■■

RIGHT ROYAL

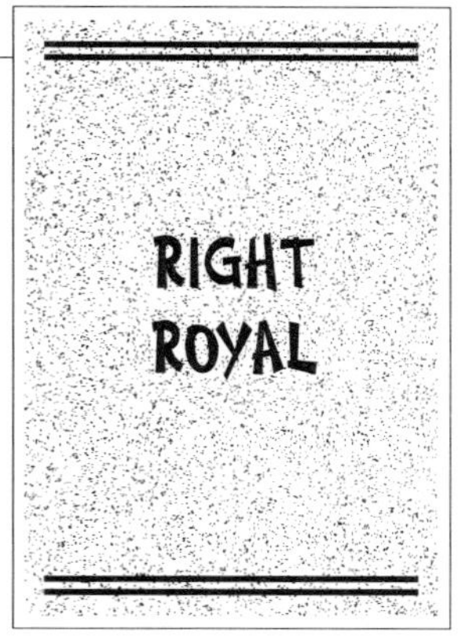

A princess was getting married in England and rumours spread in Peshawar that her parents, the King and the Queen, were giving Peshawar to her as part of her dowry. The rumour was not altogether without any foundation. This kind of thing had been happening in the days gone by when Britannia ruled the waves. The Nawab of Hoti in Mardan district of NWFP had received Hoti as part of the dowry his wife had brought to his household. And the wife's father had bought Hoti from a British prince whose wife had received it as dowry from the royal family in England.

Not far away from Hoti, some twenty miles upwards of Rawalpindi, is the lovely little hill-station of Murree. The Khan of Murree had sold that station to the local estate agents of the British Government for two "twenties" (Rs 40). He had earlier purchased it for one twenty from a royal British princess who had received it as part of her dowry from Their Majesties, the King and the Queen. After establishing their sway over the hill-station, the British had converted Murree into a cantonment and it was from that cantonment that their soldiers were keeping a constant watch on the movements of people around, those in Peshawar, Rawalpindi and Lahore included.

Peshawar could not be kicked about as Hoti and Murree. All kinds of questions were raised. What happens to us? asked the people. Shall we all be taken to England and auctioned there? Shall we be sent away to some far-away British colony in Africa and made to work as slaves there? What happens to our wealth, shops and houses, streets and bazars, temples and mosques? Men got hold of their rifles and went atop their houses, and fired shots in the air. Women assembled in the streets and beat their breasts.

Good sense prevailed in England. The princess was married, but Their Majesties, the King and the Queen, dropped the idea of giving Peshawar to her as part of her dowry. Instead, they gave her some other city or country, Falkland in Latin America or Singapore in South-East Asia.

I was not one of those who had climbed up to the top terraces of their houses to fire shots in the air to prevent Peshawar from going to some British princess as part of her dowry. Perhaps my grandfather was. He was a good shot, and could shoot down a pigeon from a distance of one mile.

A long time has gone by since Peshawar was saved the shame of being treated as a royal princess's dowry. Whose turn is it now? Britannia no longer rules the waves. But others have come in its place. They sail under strange names — G-5, G-8, G-15, G-21, and funny alphabets and digits like that. Rumours are afloat that this time they have their eyes on Kashmir. That is a place more strategic than Murree from where to keep a watch on people down below. They forget that G-strings have a knack of revealing more than what they are ostensibly intended to conceal. That apart, are we still in the age of divine rights of the kings? It looks like that.

■■

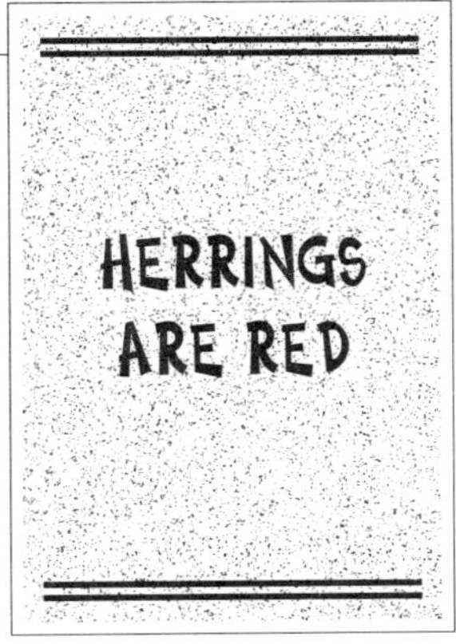

HERRINGS ARE RED

The daughter of an Indian maharaja was abducted by the son of another Indian maharaja while taking a stroll on The Mall in Shimla. This happened during the British days when there were lots of maharajas having their own little kingdoms under the protective umbrella of the king of England.

Every maharaja had his own rules. The rules in these two states, adjoining each other, were that if anyone from either of them committed a crime in the other state and escaped back to his own, no one from the state in which he had committed the crime could chase and arrest him in his own state. The police was forbidden to do that.

What to do to retrieve the maharaja's daughter from the clutches of her abductor who had escaped back into his own state? The matter was considered at various levels in the state to which the princess belonged. One difficulty involved was that the girl abducted was not the maharaja's legal daughter. She was the daughter of one of his one hundred and one concubines. The redeeming feature in the situation was that the prince who had abducted her was also not his father's legal son. He, too, was the son of one of his father's one hundred and one concubines.

Just as in these days of peak democracy, the greatness of a leader is measured by his or her lung power in Parliament and crowd-pulling power outside, the greatness of maharajas in those days was measured, *inter alia*, by the number of concubines they had. In this respect, the maharajas of both the states involved were equal. All things considered, it was decided by the commander-in-chief of the state to which the princess belonged to invade the state to which she had been abducted. In taking that decision, the

C-in-C had naturally obtained the approval of his maharaja. For the latter, decision-making was a bit difficult. What would the king's emperor in England say? But since it was a matter of *izzat*, the maharaja, after deep thought, gave the go-ahead to his C-in-C.

All preparations were made for the invasion. The troops had already been put on maximum alert. Just a little before the invasion, the C-in-C went to his maharaja and posed a highly relevant question. "Your Highness", said he, "we will go ahead as planned but who will guard us if in the course of our invasion, night falls and we go to sleep?"

I overheard this hilarious conversation between students of Himachal University in the coffee house in Shimla some 10 years ago. I had all but forgotten it. But suddenly it came back to me when I read in the newspapers that two or three millitants had sneaked into an Army base in Delhi's heavily-guarded Red Fort, and after shooting two or three jawans gone back to where they had come from.

■■

Once upon a time, not long ago, there was a governor in a certain state of India. He had three children from his first wife and another three from the woman he had married after the first one had died or deserted him. The new woman in the governor's life also had three children from her previous husband who had committed suicide.

The governor had a bright young IAS officer called Talwar as his private secretary One of his principal duties was to see that the children from the governor's first wife and those from his second wife and her first husband were kept away from the children that they had jointly produced. Talwar put the children from the governor's first wife and the governor's second wife's first husband in six different educational institutions having hostels of their own. The children jointly produced by the governor and his second wife lived with them in the Raj Bhavan.

One day, the governor received a message from the principal of the school in which one of the boys from his first wife was studying saying that the boy was going astray. Almost simultaneously, he received another message from the principal of another school in which a boy from his second wife's first husband was studying saying that the bloke had been seen roaming about in the city's red light area. The governor requested Talwar to go to both the institutions to see what was what and to try to set matters right at his own level. Talwar was also instructed to make sure that the fact of the governor's children from his first wife and his second wife's children from her first husband not behaving correctly was kept a closely-guarded secret.

Hardly had Talwar left for the two places when the governor received a message from another school in which his eldest daughter from his first wife was studying saying that the girl had tried to commit suicide. Talwar was asked to proceed to the girl's school post-haste. But as soon as he reached that school, he found another message awaiting him. It was also from the governor and it said that the governor's second wife's eldest daughter studying in a different school at a different place had been caught red-handed while stealing a gold bangle from a jewellery shop. Talwar was asked to leave the one who had tried to commit suicide and to rush to the one who had been caught stealing.

He discharged all his assignments competently and, returning home, suggested to the governor that in the interest of family harmony, it would be better if all the nine children lived together in the Raj Bhavan. That was accepted by the governor and his second wife. But, then, one day, the latter came to him and said, "Trouble again. Your children and my children are fighting furiously with our children".

I can't say what happened thereafter. But looking at the political maze, the making and unmaking of gods and goddesses, their offspring running amok, any wonder why that great gubernatorial escapade has suddenly come to mind?

■■

What do you do with all these newspapers? There was no need for me to put that question to her. For, I knew that she was using them for making paper bags. Every morning, she would come up and ask my wife for the previous day's papers. In those days, I used to subscribe to four. My wife would pass them on to her.

She was our landlord's mother. We were living on the first floor. She was living with her son, daughter-in-law and their children downstairs. There were two staircases connecting the two floors – one on the front for the rest of us and the other at the back for the maid. I had a spaniel bitch named Ruby. She knew the landlord's mother well. To her, the lady was always welcome. So was the maid. But none else would she allow to come up to the first floor through the back staircase.

Ruby's relations with the landlord were particularly strained. The fellow was all the time pressing me for increasing rent. When he would argue with me too much, Ruby would start barking at him. In retaliation, he would tamper with the supply of water to us. There were quarrels on that score. Ruby knew that. Early morning, as she would see the landlord from the balcony down below, she would bark at him without any provocation. The landlord would shout at her. The more he shouted, the more Ruby barked. Finally, things came to such a pass that the landlord gave me a notice asking me to either get rid of Ruby or to leave his house. That, however, is another story.

While Ruby did not like the landlord, she was on the best of terms with his mother. Lovable lady, shock-absorber as most mothers are, what did she do with the paper bags she made? Sadly,

I have to say that she used to sell them to one of the provision stores from where we were buying sundry household goods. She never talked about that. Nor did she talk about the treatment that was being meted out to her.

But we knew it. With her bent back, she would go to the milk-booth to fetch milk for the family. And she would cleanse the family's utensils, morning and evening. Economically weak, physically harassed, she did not want to become too much of a burden on those who were supposed to support her.

■■

Fifty years of relentless effort have been invested in bringing the prophylactic to its present level where you can ask for it across the counter and have it in all the several colours of the rainbow, each colour suiting the mood of the day. Gone are the times when I was taken to task for introducing a jingle on AIR where a woman tells her husband, "No, no, not again, I am afraid", and the husband assures her, "Nothing to worry about, darling, I have the condom with me." An all-India conference of chief ministers, represented by their media officers, had to be convened to clear that jingle.

Before me, there were other luminaries in the health ministry who had made heroic efforts to set the condom rolling in various parts of India. Bob Blake of the Ford Foundation got hold of an elephant and made it roam about all over with a scroll on its back asking the people around, "For Family Planning, Use Condom". D K Tyagi left nothing that was visible, from village mud walls to match boxes women use in kitchen, without the glorious message of Nirodh inscribed on it. The message slipped through your fingers as you picked up a pencil. It stared at you as you looked at a calendar, or as you put out the cigarette in an ash-tray.

That was all for creating favourable climate. Long after that climate had been created and several national and multi-national companies had been persuaded to sell condoms, along with their own stuff like tea, coffee and soap, through millions of sales outlets available to them, funny things started happening. In UP and Bihar, people rose up in protest saying that they were not used to wearing bathing costumes while swimming in the Ganga. In Punjab, famous for its double 'Patiala' peg, they said that they were used to doing it twice, at a stretch. How to change the condom in mid-stream?

In Kolkata, a peculiar problem arose. What to do with the used ones? "Dig up pits in the backyard of your house," said the media officer to them, "and bury the condoms deep down there, dead or alive." In Hyderabad, I ran into a doctor, a state family planning officer, who said that someone had threatened to sue him because the rubber had burst during use. The doctor wanted to know whether the GOI would stand by him in case the suit did come up.

I can't vouch for this story; it sounds somewhat exaggerated. But an old colleague, a former health ministry joint secretary now with the UNFPA, has narrated it to me. MGR was lying sick in his house in Madras. The only diversion available to him was the TV set. Day in and day out, the idiot box was throwing up ads on the darned thing. Fed up with them, MGR, whose speech was impaired, ordered a senior minister in his cabinet to remove TV at once. Promptly, a gentleman called TV Anthony was removed. He was the state chief secretary then but had earlier, in a different capacity, earned some name for pushing up condoms in Tamil Nadu.

■■

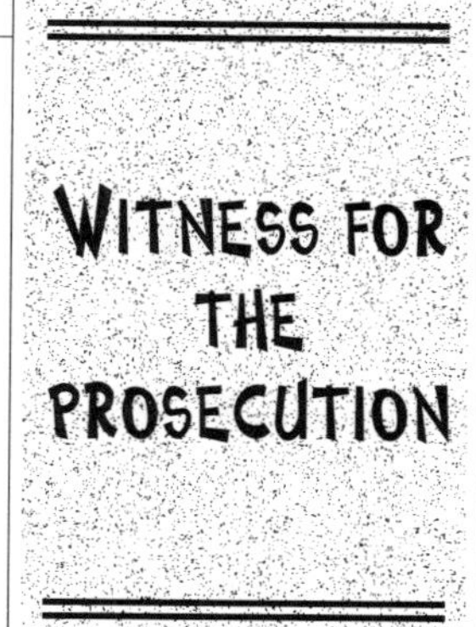

Woman in our neighbourhood fell down from the top floor of her flat. It was alleged that her husband had pushed her out of the window. Both used to quarrel every night. Both used to drink heavily.

My daughter-in-law was returning from her clinic. She saw the woman being whisked away in a car to some place. Later, we learnt that it was to a hospital she was taken. She died there or was declared brought dead.

A couple of months thereafter, Rita received summons from the court of the Additional Sessions Judge asking her to appear before the Judge on a certain date at 9 am. Since it was summons from a court, Rita had to abide by it, even though it meant loss of some practice and disappointment to a good number of her patients. I accompanied her to the Patiala House. The case did come up for hearing, though not exactly at 9. We saw the husband in handcuffs. He had been hauled up on the charge of murdering his wife. The Judge did not hear the case. Either the defence lawyer had not turned up or something else had happened. The Judge gave a new date. His clerk gave Rita a slip on the strength of which she could claim her travel allowance. On the new date, we went to Patiala House again on time. We wafted there for two long hours and discovered that the case had been adjourned again. This time, mercifully, we managed to find the payment *babu* in his seat. He made Rita sign a certain document and gave her Rs 70. "What shall I do with it," Rita said to me, "I have lost practice worth more than a thousand. And my patients must be cursing me."

Came the third time. The Judge was there but he was about to hand over charge of his office or of some of the cases to some other judge. He said to Rita that she had to come some other day. As he was about to leave, I requested him to hear me "off the record." He was kind enough to accede to my request. "Sir," I submitted to him, "what is the fault of my daughter? She has been called by your court thrice just because she had the misfortune of seeing the dead woman being whisked away?"

The Judge was kind enough to give Rita another date and to assure her that he would record her statement on that date punctually at 9 am. He did that. I can't say what happened to the case thereafter. In our housing society, a good number of people are either themselves politicians or connected with politicians. For all that I know, the case, more than four years old, is still going on. Any wonder why cases continue to pile up before courts? Any wonder why people refuse to come forward as witnesses in cases to which they may indeed be witnesses?

■■

THE FAKIR OF IPI

Between World War I that ended in 1919 and the beginning of World War II in 1939, in both of which he participated, my father spent the bulk of the years allotted to him fighting against the Fakir of IPI. He had to do that, as a part of the Indian Army.

The Fakir of IPI was the most notorious warlord of those times. The field of his operations was Waziristan and the other tribal areas around. He had managed to keep the British troops and their Indian counterparts at bay. They had control over the road running through the Khyber Pass as well as over Malakand, Swat, Swabi and half a dozen other agencies which were at par with the Indian States of those days. There, in those Agencies, the British ruled through what were known as Residents. The rest of the territory belonged to the Fakir of IPI and those who might have been his accomplices.

The British ostensibly tried their level best to capture the Fakir of IPI alive. They failed in that. Could be, they did not try hard to capture the bloke. They wanted to go on fighting the Fakir in order to keep their troops operationally fit. As far as the Fakir goes, his one great ambition in life was to shoot a British soldier dead through his mouth while the soldier was in the process of shaving his chin. The Fakir was known to be a sharp shooter. And soldiers had invariably to open their mouths in order to have a clean shave.

My father used to tell me, whenever he came to Peshawar, our home-town, that there were clear-cut instructions from the Army Command that soldiers must not perform the obligatory ritual of shaving their chin while standing or sitting on a rock in the open. They had to do it in the safe sanctuary of their barracks or field tents. Anybody detected disobeying that order could be court-martialled.

Did the Fakir of IPI achieve his life-long ambition to shoot a British soldier dead through his mouth? Did the British manage to capture him at all? I am not in a position to answer those questions for I was bundled out of Peshawar as freedom came and my father had retired earlier than August 15.

But today, as I read about the great exploits of our great hero, Koose Muniswamy Veerappan, in the forests of Karnataka, and I learn more and more about his remarkable ability to bring the government down to its knees, I can't help thinking of IPI. And I can't help thinking of our no less remarkable ability to surrender before those who have the guts to hold us to ransom.

Isn't the story of India in recent times a testimony to that? In order to gain something precious, we are ready to part with something valuable. How long can this spectacle go on?

■■

What the Talibans are doing in Afghanistan reminds me of one of my noble teachers, Ustad Maulvi. He used to teach Persian in classes IX and X in our school in Peshawar way back in the thirties. In each period, and there used to be eight periods, Ustad Maulvi would pick up four or five students and ask them difficult questions from the Persian poetry of Sheikh Saadi or Hafiz Sheerazi. On their failure to give correct or complete answers, he would give them two options – one anna fine or six canes on the palms of both hands. Invariably, the students, all coming from well-to-do families (Ustad Maulvi was quite choosy), would prefer the former. There was a tea-shop outside the school. Ustad Maulvi would send one of the boys fined to fetch a kettle of tea for him. The price was one anna. That took care of the fine imposed on the boy. The rest of the annas, imposed as fine on other boys, Ustad Maulvi would quietly slip into one of the pockets of his long coat.

Everybody knew that those annas never went to the school cashier. We did not have any such questionable system as imposition of fines on students in those days. Punishment was always in the form of canes. I cannot say how many annas Ustad Maulvi was able to collect every day. That depended on the number of periods he had in junior classes.

Lab pae aai hae dua bun kae tamanna meri; zindagi shamaa ki surat ho Khudaya meri (on my lips has come my wish in the form of a prayer; oh Lord, may my life be like that lamp which gives light to all) – that was our school prayer. Ustad Maulvi used to lead us all in reciting it every morning. He was a religious man and would offer his prayers as often as his classes permitted him.

The supply of milk to the school came from the management or the government as a sort of today's mid-day meal. The responsibility of distributing that milk to students was also assigned to Ustad Maulvi. Since not many students were fond of milk, and the quota per student was one large tumbler, almost ninety per cent of it remained unconsumed.

Where did the unconsumed milk go? Certainly not down the drain. There was no underground drainage system in Peshawar in those days. Somehow the Inspector of Schools came to know about the wastage of milk in our school. He called us all and asked us one by one whether we were getting our milk in school. Most of us honestly replied in the negative.

Ustad Maulvi was caught with his pants down. But no action was taken against him. For that was the year he had turned Haji, meaning he had returned from Haj (pilgrimage to Mecca and Madina). Not many people could afford to go on that expensive pilgrimage in those days. But Ustad Maulvi had at his disposal his annas from fines, and earnings from the unconsumed milk.

How could any punishment be given to him? If the upholders of human rights have today closed their eyes to what the Taliban are doing to women in Afghanistan, with the annas and milk they have so generously bestowed on them in the form of guns and gunships, what punishment could the management of our small school in Peshawar give in those days to a highly-respected teacher who had just acquired the distinction of being called a Haji?

■■

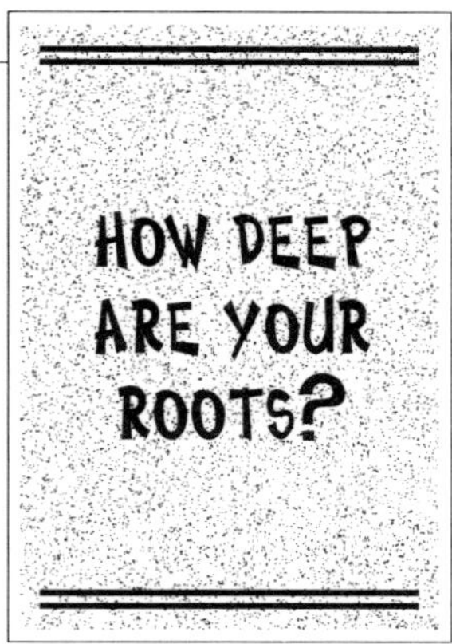

On weekends, I used to come from Sussex University in Brighton to London. It was a journey of two and a half hours by train. The fare was 2.5 pounds. I was on a paltry allowance of 4.5 pounds a day from the British Council. That was too small an amount for London. So, I would spend the night at some friend's house. The BBC was generous to me. It would give me programmes at one pound a minute. The normal broadcasting time was 10 minutes. That meant 10 extra pounds. And that was godsend.

The year was 1976. My friend, Amar Nath Arora, with whom I was staying, had planned to take me to Hyde Park. Nothing special there, but Hyde Park is Hyde Park. If the battle of Waterloo was won on the playing fields of Eton, all other battles, verbal, of course, which England has been fighting from time immemorial, have been fought and won or lost in Hyde Park. Fish and chips, costing 75 pence, was all that you needed to watch those glorious events.

It so happened that that Sunday, my friend's car refused to move. He fiddled with it, but no results. London does not work on Sunday. All workshops are closed that day. But there lived a Punjabi mechanic not far away from my friend's place. A friend in need is a friend indeed. Wherever I have gone, I have found all good Punjabis following that golden principle. My friend went to the mechanic's place. The gentleman indulged in no dilly-dallying. He came, along with my friend, in his own car. And even though he knew that the Brits who might be watching him, and there were some who did watch, would frown at him for working on a Sunday which was not in tune with whatever is meant by

British culture, he opened the car and quickly detected what was wrong with it.

Some part had worn out. He said that he had that part, a new one, at his house for emergencies like the one in which we were placed. He went home in his own car and brought the new part with him. He had all the tools that he needed and he had something much more. That something was to enable my friend to see that his friend from Brighton was not let down.

It took him no more than half an hour to replace the worn-out part and to set the car moving. As he was working on his job, he asked me all the questions Punjabis ask fellow Indians all over. When he came to know that I was from Delhi, he asked me, raising his head aside the car bonnet, whether in Delhi I got the opportunity to visit Karol Bagh. "Once in while," I answered, "I live on Pandara Road and that is a bit away." "Next time you go to Karol Bagh," said he, "do me a favour. There in Naiwali Gali no. 5 lives my mother. Kindly meet her and tell her that I am all right and that she should have no worry on my account and rather take care of her own health."

I did ask the man whether he was not in correspondence with his mother. "I am," said he, "but you have seen me in person and if you talk to her, she will be more convinced."

Forgive me, Paramjit Singh, I have not been able to go to Naiwali Gali no. 5. But I respect greatly the love that you have for your roots.

■■

It was one of those lovely evenings which the Lord gives to man out of his infinite bounty. I had gone to Malihabad, the land of the famous dassehri mangoes, the land of the famous poet, Josh Malihabadi, some 20 miles from Lucknow. There was a cultural programme there, organised jointly by the Song and Drama Division of the Government of India and the Information Department of the UP Govt I was to preside over that programme.

Hide not, oh moon, hide not, as long as I sing the song; let me sing this song of life to my heart's content. That was the first verse of one of the popular songs of those days in the mid-fifties. I think it was from a film called "Man Ki Jeet". The film was based on Thomas Hardy's Tess of the D' Urbervilles. That song provided the background music to whatever else was arranged that evening.

Dassehri mangoes used to be quite cheap. A dheri would cost just about two or three rupees. And it consisted of 33 mangoes. The top layers used to be of big ones. Below them were often the smaller ones. Typical of merchants who make millions in the sabzi mandis of India!

As the programme ended, the village biradari insisted that before leaving for Lucknow, we must have our dinner with the village gentry. That was not on our schedule. We had to return to Lucknow. And it was getting pretty late. Along with my colleagues, I tried to take leave from the village people. "Nothing doing," said their headman, an elderly Muslim gentleman in typical Lucknavi dress (chikan kurta and pyjamas), "no one comes to Malihabad as our guest and goes back from here without taking his dinner with us. We have arranged the dinner and all those who matter in the village are going to attend it".

Feeling embarrassed, getting late, I tried my level best to get leave of the people of Malihabad. I failed in my efforts. The dinner was sumptuous.

"This has been the tradition of Malihabad from the days of our aaba-o-ajdad (forefathers)," said the gracious gentleman sitting next to me, "that anyone who comes here must take dinner with us. Even Jawaharlal Nehru couldn't say 'no' to us when he came to Malihabad on one of his tours during the freedom struggle".

At the end of the dinner, as our party was leaving for Lucknow, the headman came out with another gem of generosity. "Please, for my sake," pleaded he, "for the sake of the people of Malihabad, take these baskets of mangoes with you. These are special. The trees that have yielded them were planted here by Jawaharlal and Rafi Sahib. They planted them a long time back with their own hands. And we have taken special care to see that nothing happens to those trees. Their mangoes are as sweet as mangoes from other trees in Malihabad. But the trees from which these have come are special to us".

We had to accept those baskets as gifts. The sentiments behind them were typical of the people of Malihabad. The sentiments behind them were typical of all that is best in the culture of Malihabad, and the culture of India.

Mangoes were never that sweet.

■■

They came all the way from Pittsburgh in the US to New Delhi to celebrate the 80th birthday of their mother. That would not be absolutely correct. Actually, they had come on a holiday after several years. And it so happened that their mother's birthday fell in that period. And so they decided that they should have a get-together of close relatives and old friends. They also decided, with their mother's consent, of course, that they should dispose of that old house in Greater Kailash that had been lying vacant for long. Decay was claiming it.

In the mid-1970s, Sunita and Sushil, both medicos, just married then, left for the US, as part of that great avalanche of Indian doctors that slipped into the land of their dreams. The going was tough in the beginning. They had to pass several exams and, to keep body and soul together, they had to take on several odd jobs.

Over the years, Sunita and Sushil managed to establish themselves. For long periods, they had to live apart because of job compulsions. Now Pittsburgh is their home. They don't have a common workplace. But they have a dwelling of their own. And their kids are studying at different places. All are American citizens. So are Sushil's mother and brothers who followed Sushil once he had settled there. Today they constitute a small part of the great Indian diaspora that has spread the world over.

A couple of days before the birthday reception, Sunita rang up to invite my wife and me. We had our compulsions and had to deny ourselves the pleasure of being there. But Sunita and Sushil called on us before they were to depart for the US. I was happy that during their brief stay in India, having failed to get us at the party, they did spare the time to visit us.

"How was the party?" I asked Sushil. "It was excellent", said he, "all those whom my mother knew were there. My mother was happy. So were we. But then we are going back without disposing of that house. A bargain had been struck. The deal had almost been finalised. But at the last moment, my mother backed out".

I did not have to ask him the reason why. The lady's husband's blood had gone into the making of that house. And even though he was no more, he had continued to live in it.

■■

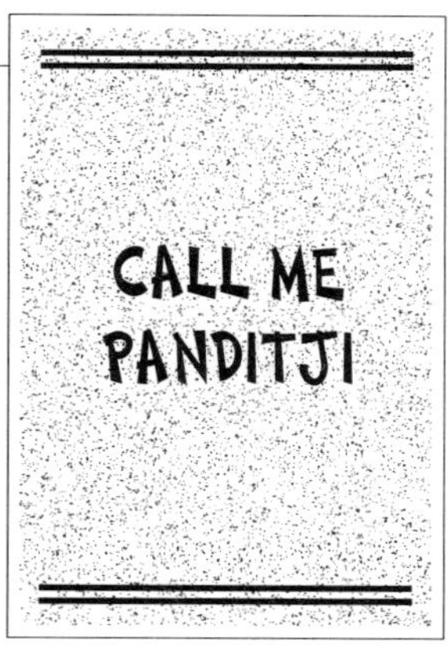

To strengthen their hold on India, the British took a fundamental decision during World War II. That was to combatise all those working as clerks in various branches of the Army. And so, barring a few exceptions, they all became NCOs (non-commissioned officers) and VCOs (Viceroy's commissioned officers). In the second category fell those who had seen long years of what is called distinguished service. They were given the venerable ranks of Jamadar Sahib, Subedar Sahib and Subedar Major Sahib.

Conversion of hard-boiled civilians into down-to-earth combatants is no joke. Numerous problems arose. Where to train them? This was taken care of by the realisation that whatever be their Army rank, babus would continue to do what babus had been doing all along. And that was pushing files in and out of trays. They had to handle no guns.

The second problem was in relation to belts and headgear. Belts were provided by the Army HQ. These came in three standard sizes – small, medium and large. It turned out that some of the babus who had become VCOs had waists too large even for the largest size in belts. For them, a new size, extra large, was improvised quickly and manufactured wholesale.

The question of headgear was somewhat ticklish. While Sikhs in all branches were as a rule allowed to wear turbans, others had to don their unit's cap. Not all the others were prepared for this. To them, turban was a symbol of "izzat". They had worn it for generations and did not seem prepared to give it up for the lowly cap. The British government, wiser by the experience of 1857, surrendered on this. Those who were absolutely devoted to the turban were allowed to go on wearing it. Others, not that bound, were given the cap.

The VCOs had to receive salute from their juniors and to give it to their seniors. That was part of the Army discipline. There was a prescribed form of salute. It had to be given and taken in a smart, tip-top fashion. For this, the right arm, along with the right hand, had to rise triangularly and the left arm had to hold the standard Army baton under its pit. All VCOs had to carry that baton with them.

We had in our unit a Subedar Major, Pandit Kanshi Ram. He had opted for the turban and had to be given the extra large belt. All through his life he had greeted people with folded hands. The Army pattern of salute was beyond him. Raising the right arm up in a triangular fashion and simultaneously expecting the left one to keep on holding the baton was too much for him.

To make matters worse, there were occasions when Subedar Major Pandit Kanshi Ram's pants rolled down. This was because the function of keeping the extra large belt tight on them, which had to be performed jointly by both hands, could not be performed properly since both were otherwise occupied. Disaster occurred one day. While smartly receiving a smart salute from a junior VCO, Pandit Kanshi Ram's baton fell down, the turban narrowly escaped following suit and the extra large belt lost its grip on his pants.

"To hell with all this," said Panditji to all his subordinates, "for God's sake don't impose this salute-valute ritual on me. Call me Panditji, as you were calling before. And greet me with folded hands, as you were greeting me in the past. I will continue doing the same."

■■

Match-fixing has been going on in India almost since the beginning of time. And there has never been anything dishonourable about it. No bookies, no brokers, no betting. Just a go-between. She, too, not always. In today's society she has lost her role. Unlike the stars in heaven that continue to determine our destiny, she has faded out. The modern, computer-guided guys and dolls have no need for her. Of course, the astrologer remains. But he is there to assist the stars and to tell you when these are in the right mood to bless match-fixing.

Sometimes it happens that the stars themselves disappear. They get drunk or drowned. That is the period when no match-fixing should be done. If the stars, on reappearance or even otherwise, discover that in their absence any match-fixing has been done, catastrophe can follow. That is, of course, preventable. The astrologer is always in intimate touch with them. He is always there to warn you when not to indulge in match-fixing.

"Wanted a good-looking manglik boy, preferably electronic engineer, from a respectable family for a manglik girl, tall and beautiful, lecturer in a well-known college, daughter of an IAS officer". That kind of colourful advertisement we see in the matrimonial columns of newspapers off and on. Who are mangliks? What happens if match-fixing is done between a manglik bay and a non-manglik girl? Catastrophe, again. What happens if a manglik boy falls in love with a non-manglik girl and the two are determined to tie the knot?

There is a solution. First, mangliks, boys or girls are those who take their birth under the influence of some ominous star. They must marry only those who have taken birth under the influence of the same star. If they marry outside the jurisdiction of that particular star, either the boy or the girl dies prematurely.

Now the solution, based on what I understand reliably from circles close to astrologers. The manglik boy or girl, as the case may be, first gets married to a peepul tree. The priest has special hymns for that kind of marriage. The peepul tree, in the course of the marriage ceremony, takes upon itself the influence of the ominous star and, therefore, the boy or the girl, as the case may be, can marry anyone of his or her choice, manglik or non-manglik. No catastrophe follows.

The peepul tree, as we all know, is immortal. It has its roots above in heaven and branches below in the world of men. I have no reason to disbelieve the astrologers when they say that approached reverentially, it can suck and absorb the pernicious influence of any ominous star. I wish those Indian cricketers who are now in trouble on account of match-fixing had known this. The peepul tree, or anything else symbolising its remarkable characteristics and simultaneously reflecting the Lord's glory might have prevented them from getting caught in the traps thrown by cheap temptations.

■■

When Prithviraj Kapoor left Peshawar for Mumbai early last century, everybody told his mother that she had lost her son to sin. Mumbai in those days was known in Peshawar, my hometown, as the city of sin. No one could imagine then that Prithviraj's journey would result in the foundation of the famous Prithvi Theatre and see the emergence of the Kapoor clan in Bollywood. From Shashi, Shammi and Raj to Randhir, Kareena and Karisma and a host of others, Mumbai owes so much to Peshawar. Prithvi was followed by Yusuf Khan (Dileep Kumar), Zakiria Khan (Jayant), Amjad Khan's father, and several others, including theatre managers.

Jawaharlal Nehru was one of Prithvi's great admirers. He nominated him to the Rajya Sabha. And it was in that capacity that I ran into him in 1960 when he was staying at the erstwhile Constitution House on Kasturba Gandhi Marg in New Delhi. I, too, was allotted a room there on my first appointment in the government of India. Naturally I went to pay my respects to Prithviraj. We were sitting in the dining hall having lunch. I went up to him and told him that I, too, was from Peshawar. From then onwards, whenever he was in the dining hall, he would call me to his table and talk to me of days gone by.

"Shall I tell you something," he said once jocularly "I really do not know what I am supposed to do in the Rajya Sabha. It was easier for me to act as Mughal-e-Azam in the film of that name than to play the role of an MP in the Rajya Sabha. God knows what Panditji saw in me. But whenever I am in Delhi and the Rajya Sabha is in session, I make it a point to attend it."

Prithviraj never allowed me to pay for my bills. He said to me bluntly that it would be highly impertinent on my part to pay for my meals when he was there. Once I had guests. He paid for them as well. "Your guests," said he, "are my guests," and then added laughing, "You know one thing, my dear boy, for your guests, you will have to pay Rs 5 per head. If they are mine, I have to pay just Rs 2.50. That is one of the many privileges I enjoy as an MP."

■■

The hon'ble chief minister knew that he was no longer needed. He was just being tolerated. He had played a glorious role in the freedom struggle. He had received lathi blows from the police during the agitation against the Simon Commission in 1919. And he had later, during the Quit India movement in the 1940s, spent four long years in the Ahmednagar Fort. But, then, his memory had started fading. He was often forgetting the names of his own ministers and calling tweedledurns tweedledees.

The other harsh fact was that one of his own colleagues, holding several portfolios, including the all-important portfolio of home, was all the time trying to find ways and means to ease him out. Ostensibly, he was on the best of terms with his chief. Whenever the two of them had to attend an important function connected with the party or the government, he would escort or receive the chief and garland him. But deep down within him, the ambition to replace the chief was simmering powerfully all the time. He knew that the chief, wise and experienced as he was, was fully aware of this.

He knew, for instance, that the home minister had set up a network of spies around him. Who comes to see the CM? When and why? What transpires between the two? Is it absolutely official or something more dangerous? Something like any move to get rid of him with the help of Delhi? Both the home minister and the chief minister had powerful supporters over there.

The home minister had one great advantage: All the intelligence agencies within the state were under him; and so he was in a better position to remain well-posted about the goings-on at his chief's residence. It was said that the peanut-seller outside the gate was indeed a secret police officer. And the chief minister knew that.

The chief minister also knew who comes to the home minister's place at what time and in what garb. What conspiracy is being hatched against him? Apart from the caller in disguise, who else is there? Has he come in an official car or a private one, or in a cycle-rickshaw? Is he a known supporter of the home minister? What has transpired between him and the man in disguise? What has transpired between the two of them and the home minister? Have they contacted Delhi? If so, whom? Did they seem to be happier after talking to Delhi?

The intelligence agencies being the monopoly of the home minister, how did the chief minister manage to remain posted with the day-to-day goings-on at the home minister's place? When was that? And where? I can't reveal all that. What I can tell nevertheless is that it was long before TV and Tehelka had invaded India. And secondly, and more importantly, both the chief minister and the minister could not get sound sleep at night without getting their heads massaged. And Monsieur Masseur for the one was the same as Monsieur Masseur for the other.

■■

Ved Mehta came all the way from New York to New Delhi to interview the health minister. From my office on the first floor of Nirman Bhavan, I went down to the portico to receive him. As he alighted from his chauffeur-driven car, he stretched forth his hand and said, "How are you, Mr Kakar?" As he walked into the health minister's room and as the health minister got up in his seat to greet him, he put it to him, "How come that you are wearing this green scarf on your head?"

The minister wanted to pour tea for him from the pot. Ved Mehta prevented him from doing that. He himself poured the tea first in the minister's cup, then in his own, and said, "How much sugar do you take?" The minister said, "One spoon." Mehta poured a spoonful first in the minister's cup, then in his own. "Milk?" asked he. "No," said the minister. Mehta put the milk-pot back in the tray from which he had picked it up.

No need to go into what took place between Mehta and the health minister. A new government under Morarji Desai had taken over in Delhi and Raj Narain was assigned the health portfolio. He had defeated Indira Gandhi in the elections to Parliament from Rae Bareli in Uttar Pradesh. And he had earned fame for his famous slogan "*Ham ne nasbandi ki nasbandi kar di*" (I have sterilised sterilisation): This was following a campaign against the mass sterilisation programme which, they say, was one of the reasons for the defeat of Indira Gandhi's party.

Lots of correspondents from USA and Europe were coming to New Delhi to interview Raj Narain. As the media chief in the health ministry, I had to be present. Ved Mehta was then on the staff of the *New Yorker*. The interview over, as he left the minister's room, I wanted to escort him down to his car in the portico. He requested me not to do that. Still, lest he should trip, I followed him, negotiating the staircase. And lest he should feel offended, I did so almost surreptitiously.

The chauffeur opened the car-door for him. Before getting into the vehicle, he shook hands with me and thanked me. Not for escorting him back but for the interview with the minister I had arranged.

How did Ved Mehta, stark blind, know that Raj Narain was wearing a green scarf on his head?

■■

Ajit Singh was a criminal lawyer. I don't know why lawyers taking up criminal cases call themselves criminal lawyers. They don't commit crime. They only defend criminals. Anyhow, that is not my concern. Hardy, who subsequently became the Chief Justice of the Delhi High Court, practised both civil and criminal law. A distant relative, I was staying with him. There was a party at his place. Some other lawyers, apart from Ajit Singh, were also present. Suddenly around midnight, Ajit Singh, after consuming three or four pegs of whisky, started weeping. What had gone wrong? Everyone present enquired.

"Bloody fools," said Ajit Singh, "you have made me drink so much that I have forgotten that I had to pick up my wife from Gurudwara Rakabganj. I had told her unequivocally that I would be there punctually at 11." Hardy consoled Ajit Singh by saying that not much was lost. He was late by just one hour.

It was Gurupurab Day. We all drove up to Rakabganj to give moral support to Ajit Singh. While we were trying to spot the lady, some policemen came forward and almost arrested us for ogling. With collars loosened, neckties hanging by them, coats thrown carelessly on their shoulders, lawyers do look like vagabonds. Ajit Singh's wife could not be located. "She must have gone home with some neighbour," said Ajit Singh, "anyhow *jithe raven, khush raven* (Live happily wherever you live)".

Back at Hardy's place, more liquor was consumed. Time came for the party to break. Alit Singh insisted that we all must accompany him to convince the lady that he was in respectable company. None was prepared for that kind of music. But since Ajit Singh was Hardy's guest, he demanded that Hardy should stand by him. And since I was staying with Hardy, on Hardy's insistence, I had to accompany the two. "*Rab khair kare, aj shamat aan wali ae* (May God be merciful! Calamity awaits me today)," said Ajit Singh, heaving a deep sigh of agony.

Hardy asked him to relax and take it easy. He had countenanced similar ordeals earlier, too, and this was all a part of the game of life. If there was no *noke-jhonk* (pinpricks) between wife and husband, conjugal life would lose all its charm. "When she goes out," said Ajit Singh, trying to appear brave, "she never tells me where she is going. Is it the duty of husbands alone to be always on time?"

Hardy said: "Certainly not. In any case, you should not be worried. I have stood by you through thick and thin and tonight, too, God willing, I will stand by you."

God was not willing. As we climbed up the staircase of Ajit Singh's flat and as Ajit Singh pressed the call bell, the door opened and from inside fell on him an unprintable shower of abuses. And with that came an unending shower of ladies' sandal. It looks Ajit Singh's wife had collected all her sandals and kept them close to the door. While Ajit Singh took the brunt of the attack, some sandals fell on Hardy, too. "Let us get out of here," said Hardy, dragging me down the staircase and murmuring to Ajit Singh at the same time, "*jithe raven, khush raven.*"

■■

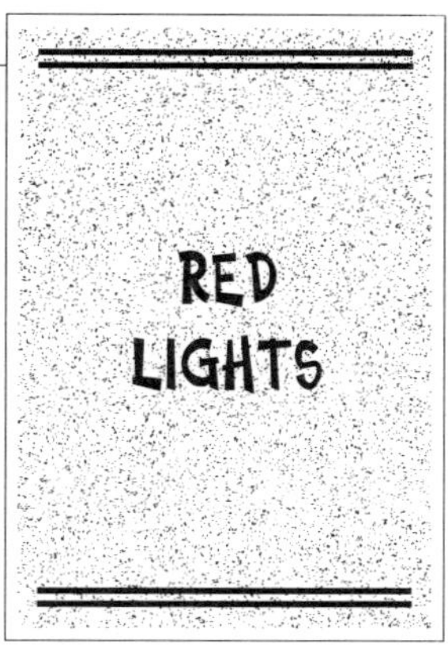

Not long ago, I was on a visit to Port Blair in the Andamans. I had gone there, delegated by the ministry of information and broadcasting, to finalise details of an exhibition-cum-cultural programme with the chief commissioner, Mr Butalia, and his highly jovial deputy, Mr Scot, a young Khasi IAS officer from Shillong. The motor car revolution had till then not overtaken India. In Port Blair, in any case, apart from government jeeps, I did not see many other cars. And yet at every road crossing, there were automatic traffic lights, yellow, green and red. One had naturally to obey the command of those lights.

"When there is not much traffic on the roads", I asked Scot, "when there are not many cars to be seen, why these traffic lights?" I recall the reply that Scot gave to me. "You know", said he, "being a Union Territory, we are governed directly by Delhi. Someone over there had decided that we needed traffic lights like Delhi itself needed them. They placed an order with a firm in Mumbai. Representatives of that firm came here and selected the spots where we must have those lights. Since we did not have to pay for them and since we did not want Delhi to think that we were backward and since in our heart of hearts it also occurred to us that automatic traffic lights did indeed add to the glory and prestige of a town, we agreed readily.

"That apart, who the dickens are we to question the wisdom of Delhi? It is blokes over there who determine our needs. And it is they who find ways and means to meet them. We dutifully do what they ask us to do. After all, he who pays the piper, calls the tune".

"Of course", added Scot, "our basic needs, as they call them, are altogether different. For instance, we have been requesting

Delhi to increase the number of flights from Kolkata to Port Blair from two to three a week. And to introduce better aircraft so that in the event of clouds or things like that over Port Blair, one does not have to divert to Rangoon and get stranded over there at the airport. Besides, for years, we have been pressing for a hospital. There is a radio station here, which passes on to us whatever comes from Delhi, but there is no hospital. My wife's specs have broken. I had to send them to Kolkata for repair. God knows when these will come back from there. And when these come, will she be satisfied with them? I mean, what if the lenses don't fit into the rims correctly? Shall I have to send them back to Kolkata?"

We were going to meet the chief commissioner in Scot's jeep. Mercifully, the age of red and blue lights, some rotating, some with ear-piercing sirens, fixed atop government vehicles, racing at break-neck speed, creating helter-skelter and chaos all round, had till then not swept the country off its feet.

■■

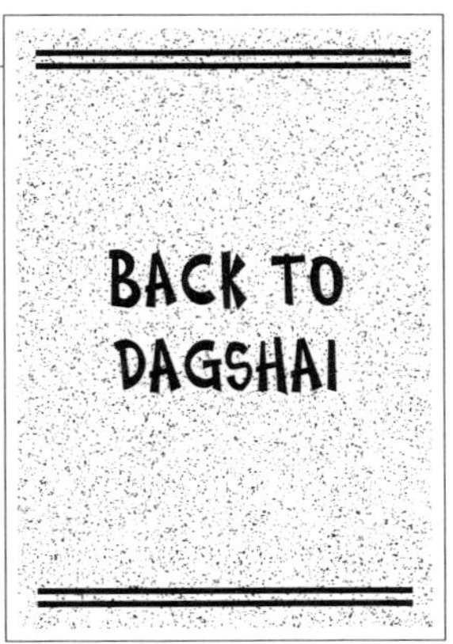

BACK TO DAGSHAI

As the car would leave Shimla for Kalka, it was obligatory that the transport officer in Shimla should inform his counterpart in Kalka accordingly. That was to make sure that the latter did not allow any car to leave Kalka for Shimla till the one from Shimla had reached there. The 56-mile-long road could take only one car at a time. It had a narrow width.

The same was the case with the small-gauge Kalka-Shimla train. There was a single track and there were too many tunnels. The longest one was near Barogh. It was almost a mile long. When no train was coming or going, pedestrians were allowed to walk through it. Huge mirrors used to be placed at the mouths of the tunnel on both sides. When the sun, was up, its rays would pierce through the tunnel and light the path for pedestrians.

Between Kalka and Shimla, there is a small hill station, Dagshai, perched on a mountain-top. It was a cantonment town and headquarters of the Royal Indian Army Service Corps (RIASC) in which my father was serving as an officer. It had no railway station of its own. One had to climb the zigzag mountain-path from Kumharhati to reach it. Our house was right in the middle of the main bazaar. Sitting in the balcony, we used to watch the Ram Lila down below. Corncobs were available in abundance, a paisa a piece, I suppose. Army families from other parts of the cantonment would join us in seeing the Ram Lila.

That was way back in the 1930s. This summer, on a holiday in Shimla, I decided to go down to Dagshai. I very much wanted to see that lovely little cantonment and the house in the bazaar in which we used to live. So I went, accompanied by my wife and daughter. The house-owner was kind enough to show us all the rooms. He helped me climb up through the window in the kitchen to the corrugated, slanting roof-top from where we used to push the snow down into the bazaar.

Two differences I noticed in the house. One, like the bazaar, it was electrified. Two, it had a water tap of its own. And, of course, unlike in the past, I did not see any policeman in the bazaar itself. The old British military police was gone for ever.

■■

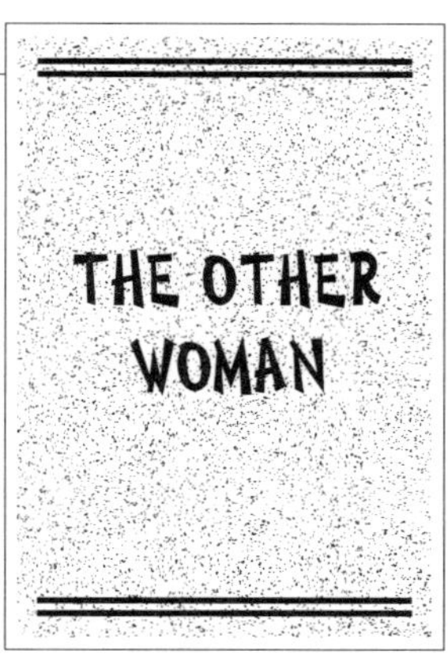

Good old Sidhu Malik was a group captain in the Indian Air Force. On his retirement in 1969, which also happened to be the birth centenary year of Mahatma Gandhi, he was very much in need of a job. A veteran in public relations, who had served the country well in Congo, the Gandhi Centenary Committee took him on as its executive director for running two exhibition trains on the life of the Mahatma all over India.

In my capacity as the exhibition chief (some called it chief exhibit) of the Information and Broadcasting Ministry's DAVP, I was the committee's honorary adviser. Dr Sushila Nayar was its president.

Those were the days when people still remembered the Mahatma. Kanu Gandhi, the well-known artist from Ahmedabad, had done him good justice through an exhibition he had designed. For a whole year, the two exhibition trains smoothly ran over the railway network. Wherever these halted, big crowds flocked to the railway stations to see the exhibition laid inside.

President V V Giri had inaugurated one of the two trains at Amritsar on Oct. 2, 1969. I can't forget that memorable day. I needed a stenographer to dictate a Press release. The deputy commission very kindly provided me his own. But he turned out to be a "gheechu-meechu". That is the Gurmukhi word for stenographer and the man could take dictation in no language other than Gurmukhi. When I pointed this out to Dr Sushila Nayar, she rightly said that that was my headache.

Of course, it was. Anyhow, everything turned out well. The benign government gave me a suitable award for that. But even more rewarding was what I received from Dr Sushila Nayar herself. She organised a farewell party at her residence on the Balwant Rai Mehta Marg. Sidhu had arrived on the scene earlier.

He had to look after the arrangements. I came a bit late. Sidhu's wife was with me. Dr Sushila Nayar mistook the gracious lady for my wife and introduced the two of us to the august Gandhian assemblage as husband and wife.

I tried hard to convince Dr Sushila Nayar that Sidhu's wife was not my wife. But the lady's mind was elsewhere. Besides, she was a bit hard of hearing. She went on introducing Mrs Sidhu as Mrs Kakar to whosoever we ran into. Sidhu's wife felt embarrassed. So did I. But both of us took the situation gallantly.

It so happens now that the Tara Apartments in which I live are named after the mother of Dr Sushila Nayar who is one of the founding members of the cooperative society owning them. Dr Sushila Nayar spends most of the year in Sewagram. Once in a while, she comes to these flats. She has her own flat here.

When she comes and per chance we run into each other, she asks me invariably, "How is Mrs Kakar?" I tell her, "She is fine," knowing not which Mrs Kakar she is referring to: the genuine one, or the widow that Sidhu, now sadly no more, has left behind.

■■

MY SISTER, SHASHI

That day, in 1967, a formidable crowd from my home-town, Peshawar, descended on our house in New Delhi's Patel Nagar to tell me that there was nothing wrong with the boy and his father was not at all greedy.

They could not convince me. For I had seen the boy dead drunk the previous week, on the occasion of the marriage of his own sister.

That same evening, his father had, in a crude, unashamed manner, pumped into my ears the loaded statement that someone else was also interested in his son and had offered to him Rs 25,000 cash in advance.

"Why don't you accept the offer?" I asked him angrily.

"Because," he quipped clownishly, "I have already given my word to you."

"Who is that someone who has offered to you Rs 25,000?" I enquired.

He had no answer to the question. Apparently there was none. Apparently also, the hint to me was that Rs 25,000 was the market price of his son and I would have to pay up the sum.

My younger sister had been engaged to the boy a few months earlier. My mother was alive. Her own younger sister was related to the boy's father from her husband's side. She had known the family very well and had testified to its decency. I had also met the boy and his parents. I did not see anything wrong in them.

But almost immediately after the engagement, hints about their expectations started pouring in. As the marriage date drew nearer, we had in hand an awkward list which included a TV set, a refrigerator and a scooter. Worse still, reports came to me that the boy was given to gambling and drinking. In a drunken state, he had smashed the mirror in a barber's shop because the barber had refused to give him preference over other waiting customers so the stories said.

The breaking point came on the night his sister was married. We called off the engagement. A week later, when the party arrived, I greeted them with respect, but I refused to yield.

They pleaded with my mother. She said that she had left everything to me. Finally the gentlemen departed, telling us that the boy's parents would return all that we had given to them at the engagement and the *shagan* ceremonies. Nothing of the sort happened.

My sister was married to another boy and my mother had the satisfaction to see her happily settled in life. By dint of her hard and dedicated work, she has made her mark in life. Before her marriage, she had joined the All India Deaf and Dumb Federation. There she learnt and mastered the sign language. She helped the organisation in setting up an arts studio and a crafts workshop for the handicapped. It was with her help that Doordarshan started a special bulletin for the deaf and dumb two years ago.

Last March, I was proud to see that little girl, Shashi Paul, now a grandmother, receiving the President's Award for her services to the handicapped. Paradoxically, the award included a cash prize of Rs 25,000.

■■

Don't believe me, for I have stopped believing in myself. No, I am not insane. Nor do I suffer from amnesia. I know it is Tuesday today and yesterday was Monday and tomorrow will be Wednesday. But one more incident of the type in which I was involved today, and from then onwards every day for me will be the doomsday.

I was driving towards Palam on the Ring Road when suddenly I was 'Marutised'. The little thing came from behind and overtook me from the left. That was its fundamental right. But then it swerved rightward, forcing me to do the same till I hit the pavement dividing the road into two parts. Nothing happened to the Maruti. It straightened up and dashed away, leaving me confused and dazed.

My car was damaged. I came out of it and tried to catch the Maruti's number. I could read only the four broad digits, but the titbits along with them – DL2CA, 3CA or ABCD – I just could not capture. I chased the damsel but it ran away. A police patrol van was parked under a tree. I approached it. The officer in charge wanted to have the complete number of the culprit.

I said that it was a white Maruti and while I was certain about the four broad digits, I could not say anything about the titbits. He was kind enough to assure me that despite that, he would splash messages. I requested him to register the FIR. He said that that could be done only at the police station, adding, at the same time, that without complete information, they might not register the case.

Someone knew some high-up in the police. I talked to him. He in turn talked to the SHO of the police station concerned. When I reached there, I received a sort of VIP treatment. The police official listened to me patiently and asked his constable to prepare the FIR.

As he was doing so, an Air Force officer walked in. His scooter had been stolen and recovered. He had identified it earlier and had been asked to bring the necessary papers to take the delivery.

"Where is my scooter?" asked the Air Force officer. "I just saw it being taken out of the police station by a man. A woman was sitting on the pillion seat."

"Must have been taken out for trial," said the police official nonchalantly.

"What trial?" demanded the AF officer. "How can you take a recovered scooter for trial?"

"The police can take out anything for trial," replied the official, "have patience; you will get your scooter soon."

I do not know when the AF officer got back his scooter.

But there was no delay in the preparation of my FIR. It was in Hindi. I could read it only when I reached back home.

It made no mention of the Maruti car but said that a cow had come my way and in order to avoid dashing against it, I had swerved to the right and hit the pavement!

Was it a Maruti or a cow? Do cows carry number plates at their back? I am puzzled. Probably there was no accident at all and I went to the police station just for a chit-chat.

■■

Can a lemon cause a communal riot? It almost did in Delhi way back in 1977. The fault was not that of the lemon. It had been kept in cold storage longer than it could stay there. As a result, it lost its juice without losing its appearance and thus exposed itself to the charge of being an agent provocateur.

The real culprit was a car, an official car. It is my belief that if we say goodbye to all the cars in India, there will be less of communal tension and more of national integration. Besides, our economy as well as our bus services will improve immensely. But since the car has come to stay with us, we cannot throw it away lock, stock and barrel. We can nevertheless cut down its use by the officialdom drastically.

Imagine the number of official cars that are engaged in what goes by the name of service of the people. If we take the development block as a unit and count only ten cars per unit, their number will exceed 50,000 since the number of blocks is over 5,000. Add to it the cars of various departments, from agriculture to astronomy, and of Ministers, you may come to the conclusion that there are nearly a million official cars promoting the people's welfare.

The figure is dazzling. It becomes shocking when we know that there is not a single official car that is not being misused. Which is that officer who will risk a war with his wife by refusing to drop her in the market while going to his office in an official car? And which is that Minister who can say with his hand on his chest that he has never used his staff car for political purposes?

I once saw staff car being sent from Dharasu in Garhwal hills to Hardwar, some 70 kms downward, to fetch a Banarsi *paan* for a very important Minister. On a pilgrimage to Uttarkashi, which he must have undertaken for the salvation of India's soul, he stopped for the night at Dharasu. The authorities concerned organised a lavish dinner for him. Everything was there, from soup to sweets, but the *paan* was missing.

Now there is hardly an Indian town which does not have a *paan* shop. Dharasu, too, has several *paan* shops. But the problem arose when it was discovered that the Minister took no *paan* other than the Banarasi one and this was not available in Dharasu as well as in the areas around. And so the car was sent to Hardwar to pick up Banarsi *paans* for him. It is another thing that by the time it returned from Hardwar, the Minister had gone to sleep.

Coming back to the lemon and the riot that it almost caused in Delhi, as I said, the culprit in the case was an official car. A minister's wife had sent it all the way from Akbar or Prithvi Raj Road in New Delhi to the subzimandi in Old Delhi to fetch half a dozen fresh lemons. When the car returned, the lady discovered that the lemons were not sufficiently juicy.

These were sent back to the same shopkeeper in the same car. A row developed between the shopkeeeper and the driver. The two belonged to two different communities. Mobs collected on both sides. Timely intervention by the police saved the situation.

Abolish the official car and promote communal harmony. That should be our national motto. If we adopt it, life for all of us is bound to be more peaceful. I have not the slightest doubt about this.

■■

Why do we immerse the ashes of our dead in the waters of some holy river? Why do we bury their bodies?

The questions are too deep for me. It will, therefore, be presumptuous on my part to go into them. After ail, as Henry Adams says, man knows mighty little and may some day learn enough of his own ignorance to fall down and pray. I am not even half aware of my ignorance.

Whatever little I know, I know on the basis of my own experience. And that tells me that when I die and my body is burnt in accordance with the prescribed rituals, my ashes should never be taken to that holiest of holy places called Hardwar.

I like the place. I have been to it and to places beyond a number of times. And I respect the value Indians place on Ganga *jal*. In earlier days, they used to carry a bit of it to England whenever they went there. Even today some families keep it. There must be something noble behind this tradition.

But what I don't like about it and about Hardwar is its gross misuse in that town by everyone, from priests to rickshaw-wallahs. There seems to be an unholy alliance among them. Cheat the relatives of the dead – that seems to be their motto.

My father died. Accompanied by my wife, I took his flowers, as we used to call them back home in Peshawar, to Hardwar. My mother had lovingly mixed a small particle of gold in them. That was the custom in our parts. It epitomised love, respect and all the other great values that have enriched the Indian culture.

We left Delhi by the early morning bus. The moment we reached Hardwar, a number of priests mobbed us. How did they discover the purpose of our visit? The casket containing my father's flowers was in a bag which I carried. We certainly could not have looked like tourists but then everybody asked the same questions: "Wherefrom, what caste; Khatri, Arora, Kapur, What?" They wanted to take charge of the ceremony in order to fatten themselves.

The rickshaw-wallah who took us to Kankhal, where the flowers were to be consigned to the holy waters, gave us a long lecture on cheating prevalent in Hardwar. When he brought us back from Kankhal to Har-ki-Pauri, he charged us more than the fare between Delhi and Hardwar.

At Kankhal, the priest who conducted the ceremony, hypnotised me completely. With the recitation of every shloka, he asked for money in the name of my father's soul. I had to go on shelling it down. He did not allow the particle of gold to get lost in water. His eyes were too sharp and hands too deft to miss it.

The priest at Har-ki-Pauri, which was the last stage in our rituals and where we took our bath and prayed, asked us to bring four kilograms of *ladoos* from the shop of the halwai opposite. We obeyed, and then did whatever else he ordained. Countless times, he asked us to bow in the name of gods and goddesses unknown to us, and every time we did so, we had to part with heavy sums of money. Out of the *ladoos* we had brought, he gave us two and then asked for his *dakchina* which, too, we had no alternative but to offer.

At the end of it all, as we sat for our lunch in the *dhaba* next to the same halwai's shop, we saw a little boy coming from the side of the temple bringing the same *ladoos* back to the halwai. The bag containing them was the same, the one in which the halwai had put the *ladoos* for us. It was so easily recognisable.

We left the *dhaba* and came back to Delhi by the first available bus.

■■

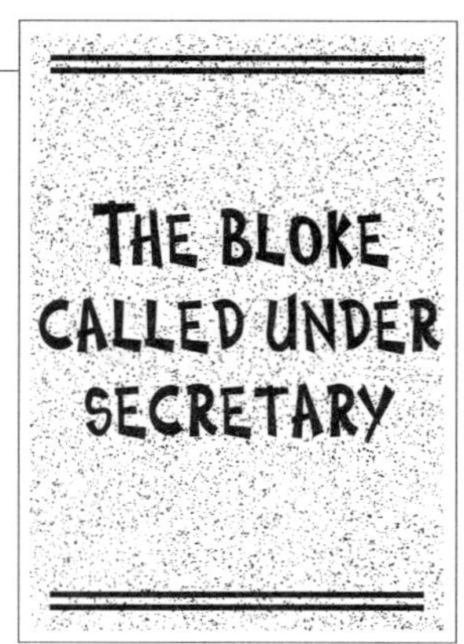

Out of every three who retire, only one will be replaced, is the latest edict from the government. But what about ninety out of every one hundred who are not needed? Think of it. What does the under secretary do? A vital link between the section officer and the deputy secretary, a hurdle as unnecessary as a second nose on a man's face, as difficult to cross as to abolish.

While working in the government, I had to fiddle with him once. Provocation – sitting in Delhi, I failed to anticipate that riots would suddenly erupt in faraway Hailakandi in Assam.

I was then the exhibition chief (some called me chief exhibit) in what unto this day is known as the Directorate of Advertising and Visual Publicity, DAVP, V for Visual but always rightly mistaken for Usual. The under secretary was above me in the sense that he was the GOI (Ministry of I&B) and I was in a subordinate office at par with AIR, Doordarshan, Press Information Bureau and things like that. He being the GOI, all my proposals had to be cleared by him: When I proposed that an exhibition should be arranged in Hailakandi, he raised a vital question: Why Hailakandi? Why not Siliguri?

I explained the reasons. He accepted them, after a bit of cross-examination. The exhibition unit, stationed at Guwahati, was directed to move to Hailakandi. And it moved. Suddenly over some cow or bull, mosque or mandir, all hell broke loose in that town. The DAVP unit had to retreat to Guwahati. The expenditure on its to-and-fro movement was declared as infructuous by the under secretary and I was called upon to explain why I should not be held responsible for it.

How the dicknens could I smell what was going to happen in Hailakandi? The under secretary's view was that as a responsible officer, I should have known that. If I had known that, I would have informed the Home Ministry.

The under secretary did not accept that view. Up and down the file moved umpteen times between Shastri Bhavan and Kasturba Gandhi Marg jhuggi-jhaunparis in New Delhi where my office was.

Months passed. The drama went on and it would have continued "from here to eternity" till one day the same bloke called under secretary was transferred from the ministry to the DAVP as my deputy. The two posts were equivalent and transferable.

I passed on the Hailakandi file to him and asked him to reply to the man who had replaced him as under secretary in the ministry and who had, like his predecessor, continued to indulge in the glorious pastime of unearthing from me the real truth behind Hailakandi.

The bloke, smarting over his conversion from the GOI's under secretary to my deputy, dutifully took up cudgels on my behalf. He filed every reminder that came from the ministry.

"Why don't you send them a reply?" I asked him naturally.

"In such cases," said he, "no reply is the best reply. That is the GOI's way I have learnt over a long period of time."

■■

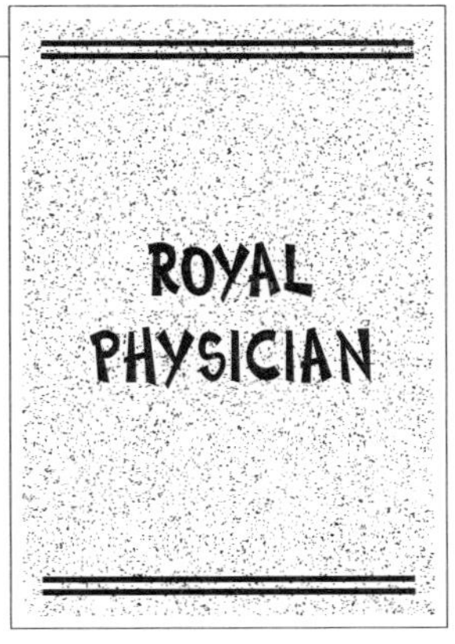

Anyone under the influence of some ominous star? Anyone on whom has fallen the shadow of a woman that has produced a stillborn babe? Anyone who has been cursed by a *kaljibi* (woman with a black tongue whose curses had devastating effects)? Anyone on whom someone has cast an evil eye? Call Bhai Nathu Singh. He had a cure for all kinds of mysterious diseases.

Men and women apart, Bhai Nathu Singh had a cure for houses, too. Houses that were infested with ghosts. Houses from which strange frightening sounds came at the dead of the night. Bhai Nathu Singh had two kinds of treatment. He would subject his patient – man, woman or house – to a recitation of his mantras. Then would come his famous pudiya (powder wrapped in paper). Human beings had to swallow the powder with milk. Houses had to absorb it in all their nooks and corners.

Bhai Nathu Singh's treatment was always considered to be highly efficacious. People from all over Peshawar used to flock to him. They came not just for those mysterious diseases but also for conventional ones like ache in the head or pain in the stomach. Bhai Nathu Singh's big, black, oblong pills were considered to be particularly effective in controlling cholera.

Every Kumbh mela, Bhai Nathu Singh used to go all the way from Peshawar to Hardwar. Not just for pilgrimage, but, more importantly, to treat people suffering from cholera. That disease generally broke out at the mela. That disease always found Bhai Nathu Singh at Hardwar, administering his famous black pills to those afflicted by it. He cured thousands.

Stories of his success spread far and wide. And in course of time, these reached the Whitehall in London also. The secretary of state, who used to rule India from over there, advised the viceroy to convey the appreciation of his majesty's government to Bhai Nathu Singh for the yeoman service he had been rendering to humanity.

And so, one day, a letter came to Bhai Nathu Singh. It was marked 'On His Majesty's Service'. Bhai Nathu Singh was frightened. He thought that some summons had come to him from the *kacheri* (court) on the complaint of someone on whom his pills had produced some adverse effect. But when the meaning of the letter was explained to him, Bhai Nathu Singh jumped with joy.

God knows who suggested it to him, but soon thereafter we saw a big placard hanging on the wall behind him inside his small shop. It carried that letter and below it announced in bold letters in Urdu and English, 'Bhai Nathu Singh's famous black pills for cure of cholera. Recognised by His Majesty's Government in England'.

Bhai Nathu Singh never charged any money from anyone. Senior to me in age by decades, he must have by now become a dear departed soul. And he must have carried with him the secret of the ingredients that went into the making of his pills.

■■

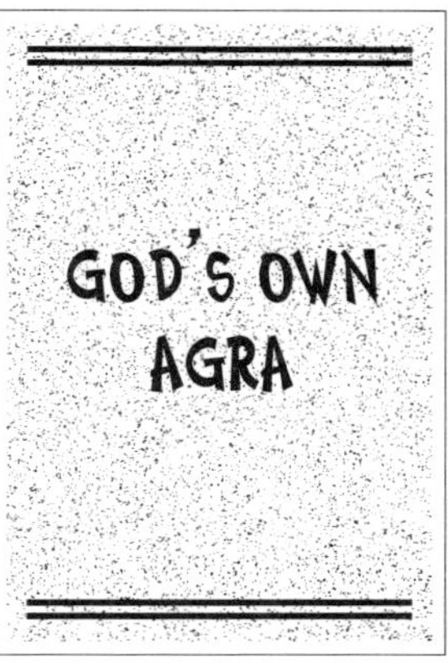

God's Own Agra

Somewhere in one of the main bazars of Agra, there was a famous restaurant called Subhan Allah. I used to take my meals there as often as I visited Agra. And I visited the city at least once every month. I visited it every time some monarch or other dignitary came to India. Invariably, he would be taken to Agra to see the Taj. And, invariably, I would be there to cover his visit.

That was in the 1950s. I was working as information officer in Lucknow, and Agra fell within my jurisdiction. I remember it was always a problem to get some place in any of the government guest houses to spend the night. The circuit house was out of bounds. It used to be taken over by the higher-ups as well as the special police that would come from Delhi to provide security cover to kings and queens, presidents and prime ministers. I always managed to get back to Lucknow by the night train via Tundla after the visit.

How many days I must have spent at the Taj in those days? And there I would recite Sahir Ludhianvi's verse on the Taj. The stanza that I liked in particular from that poem said something like this: "My beloved, don't meet me at the Taj. Meet me somewhere else. For the Taj is a symbol of how a king has mocked at the love of the poor with the backing of his great wealth".

After sending my despatch to PTI to which I was accredited as a result of a strange but highly convenient arrangement between the news agency and the government, I used to move over to the Subhan Allah restaurant to take my meals. For just rupee one, I could get a plate of mutton and two *rumali rotis*. That was highly satisfying. One evening, I saw, in addition to Subhan Allah, another restaurant called Insha Allah, just opposite it. I walked into it. For the same kind of lunch, mutton and *rumali rotis*, it charged me the same amount. "I thought you would charge me less?" I said to the proprietor. I can't forget the answer he gave. "Subhan Allah", said he, "too, belongs to our family. We have now opened Insha Allah to provide some competition and to break the monotony of Subhan Allah. Meat is cooked in the same kitchen. *Rumali roti* is also prepared at one place. Does the meat taste different?"

No, it didn't, and I said so. The gentleman was pleased to hear what I said. I didn't ask him why he had named the new restaurant Insha Allah. For I knew that while Subhan Allah meant 'The Lord is great', Insha Allah meant 'God willing'.

Years have gone by. Away from the government's information hierarchy, I have not visited Agra again. But I do hope that Subhan Allah and Insha Allah over there are doing pretty well, getting their mutton and *rumali rotis* from the same kitchen, though the rates must be up and beyond the reach of mortals like me.

■■

These are the days of quiz programmes. The biggest of them all is *Kaun Banega Crorepati*. Whether you like it or not, if you are at home, you watch it. And you wring your hands in despair when someone fails to give a correct answer to the simplest of questions. You could have done it better. You could have walked away with Rs 12.5 lakh, if not 25. But then...

Watching the programme the other night, my mind went back to the mid-70s and to the handsome prizes we had offered to shopkeepers in Delhi for trying to do something they were not accustomed to do. We took advantage of man's appetite for fame and wealth and for displaying both.

Our purpose was quite patriotic. We had to bring the condom out of its odious past when it was called FL and associated with prostitution into the modern age where, so we thought, it was destined to play a great role in the highly important national programme of family planning.

I was the media chief in the Ministry of Health and Family Welfare at that time. We rechristened the condom and gave it a respectable name – Nirodh. And we roped in nearly a dozen national and multinational marketing companies to help us in promoting it as such. They had more than half a million sales outlets at their disposal.

These outlets, small shops, were selling all kinds of things, from sanitary towels to soaps, toothpastes to torch-cells. Why not persuade them to sell Nirodh as well? We offered them high profits, more than a hundred per cent. In addition, we offered them attractive gifts such as briefcases, purses, flasks, fountain-pens and so forth. A bright young advertising whizkid suggested that we organise a display competition in some of the selected sales outlets.

Let the ministry supply them appropriate material – posters, buntings, leaflets, tinplates and all that – and let the shopkeepers themselves arrange their display artistically, for which the ministry would give out prizes.

The suggestion was accepted. The display material was designed and produced quickly. The marketing companies selected the outlets, beginning with those in Delhi. They formed their own juries. The ministry provided the necessary funds – one lakh for the best display, Rs 50,000 for the second and Rs 25,000 for the third. There were consolation prizes as well.

A couple of months, after that, I walked up to the shopkeeper who had won the first prize. When he had no other customers around, I asked him for a packet of Nirodh. "We don't sell condoms here," he said wryly. "Why?" I asked. The reply he gave was devastating. "Sir, because of that competition the government forced on me, I have been branded as a condomwallah. My regular customers for sundry goods have stopped coming to me. They do not want to be seen outside my shop. With great difficulty, I have been able to win them back. I don't want to get involved in any hanky-panky thing any more."

Watching the KBC, I could not help recalling that experience. And I wondered why Nirodh has taken so long to emerge on the Indian scene. Can those behind its promotion draw some lessons from KBC?

■■

Once on a weekend holiday in Lahore, I walked into the room of my buddy, Khan Chand Duggal, in the Ewing Hall hostel of the Forman Christian College. I had never stayed with him earlier. At the end of the Anarkali bazar, there used to be the Majestic Hotel. It was owned by a friend of my father, Bhai Wazir Singh. I had always stayed there whenever I visited Lahore, and I visited Lahore off and on. If I had not stayed with Bhai Wazir Singh, he would have felt offended and as a consequence thereof, I would have been court-martialled by my father, an army officer, who believed as much in maintaining discipline at home as in having the best of relations with his friends.

Khan Chand was taken by surprise. I remember, it was a holiday in the college because it was the day of the Basant festival. Khan Chand decided to take me to the Lawrence Garden. He had naturally one cycle of his own. He borrowed another boy's cycle for me and the two of us went on a jolly good jaunt. In the Lawrence Garden, there was a mount. We sat there together sipping Pilsner beer, eight annas a bottle. Since we were not that much used to it, we became a bit tipsy after two or three glasses. We roamed about in the garden looking at young couples embracing each other, something for which Lawrence Garden was duly famous. Late in the evening, staggering somewhat, picking up our cycles, we pedalled back to the Ewing Hall.

"Where are you staying?" asked Khan Chand. "With you, of course, where else?" said I. He was taken aback. "But you can't stay with me," said he, "for that, I have to take special permission from the warden in advance. Normally, guests are not allowed to stay with boarders at night."

Khan Chand could not have thrown me out of the hostel. And it was too late for him to knock at the door of Dr Schyler, the formidable American warden. The two of us shared the cot that Khan Chand had in his room. The next day, early in the morning, I moved back to Ferozepore cantonment, where I was stationed. But my night out in Lahore was noted by the khansama and the dining room bearer. One of them or maybe someone else, let Khan Chand down. He reported my nocturnal stay with him to the warden. And two days later, Khan Chand informed me through a letter that he had been expelled from the hostel.

"When to the sessions of sweet silent thought; I summon up remembrance of things past; I sigh the lack of many a thing I sought," – in those moments of solitude, Khan Chand is one of those who creep in quietly. He retired as a Colonel from the army and died one evening in New Delhi's Defence Colony while giving a push to a stranded car belonging to someone unknown to him. He should not have done it. For he was a heart patient. But, then, he was Khan Chand. And the likes of him leave behind on the sands of time footprints which time itself cannot wipe out.

■■

On August 25, 1991, my elder sister, Kamla, came to tie rakhi round my wrist and as usual, we talked about our native place, Peshawar. Both of us were above 20 when Pakistan was created and so we remember much about life in our old town. "How was it," Kamla asked, "that women in Peshawar managed to produce so many children?"

We were ourselves nine – seven sisters and two brothers. But there were others whose number exceeded a dozen. There was at least one woman who produced 22. It was said that on one occasion when she became pregnant and called her mother to look after her, she discovered that the latter, too, was pregnant. Who looked after whom? I do not know.

During the last elections in Pakistan, some Pakistani wags described Mrs Benazir Bhutto, leader of the Pakistan People's Party (PPP), as the permanently pregnant Premier. That was uncharitable. The remark could, however, apply to the women of Peshawar. Their state was one of perpetual pregnancy. And I suspect that they enjoyed this condition marvellously. Other things apart, it meant (a) no hard work and (b) lavish food which included a chicken a day.

During this period and the mandatory 40 days that followed it, they seldom cooked food at home. The fast food age came long thereafter, but in Peshawar, there were scores of small *dhabas* from which one could get *tikkas*, *kababs* and roasted chicken as well as crisp *naans*. Surprising though it may seem today, even milk was not boiled at home. It used to come from the *halwai*. Door-delivery was the common form.

Most of the women were quite well off. They had bricks, not biscuits, of gold locked up in their safes. Their families, on both sides, owned lots of property. The women themselves could recite *Gita* and *Gurubani* fluently but by and large they were illiterate. They could not count beyond twenty.

In those days, silver rupees were in vogue. Women used to keep these rupees in large steel trunks which were supposed to be protected by king cobras and, therefore, kids were not allowed to go near them. I remember that for every 20 rupees that my maternal grandmother put in her trunk, she used to draw the figure of one in chalk on top of it. Twenty such figures meant $20 \times 20 = 400$ rupees.

Whenever my grandfather needed extra money for the tavern to which he used to go every evening, he would take out 20 rupees from the trunk and just wipe off one figure from its top. And the man and the woman continued to live happily as long as they lived.

"Wasn't life better for women in those days?" I asked my sister.

A deeply religious lady, Kamla retorted quickly, "it was hellish. But there was one great thing. Nobody could dare burn a bride for bringing less dowry."

■■

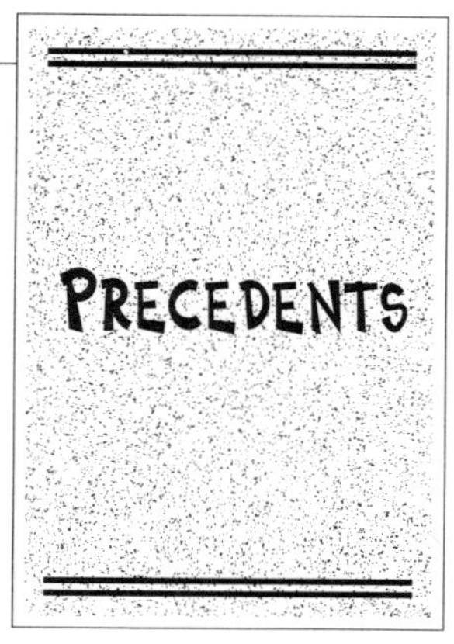

When I bade good-bye to the Government in 1981, one of the many things I had to surrender was my passport. It so happened that almost immediately thereafter, I received an offer of assignment as consultant from the Asia-Pacific Institute of Broadcasting Development in Kuala Lumpur. Without a second thought, I accepted the offer.

It did not occur to me then that I was without a passport. The institute wanted me to join it immediately to organise a course in Programme production for film and TV executive from ten countries.

Without a passport, I could not go. So I dashed to the passport office. The officer there, a charming young IFS lady, was very nice. She gave me a form and also the assurance that receiving it back, duly filled in, she would process it expeditiously.

I filled the form, got it attested and handed it to the lady the same day. She asked me to come back after a fortnight to collect my new passport. That, she added, was the minimum period required; the normal period was four to six weeks.

I could not wait that long. The course was to begin in a week's time. I pleaded with her to use her discretionary powers and waive whatever formalities she could possibly waive. She said that she had already taken that into consideration and reassured me that she would personally see to it that no delay occurred at any point.

I was at may wit's end. I did not want to lose the opportunity to go to Kuala Lumpur but it seemed to be evading me. After the passport, I had to get the vias. That could easily take two days. I tried a number of officers in the Ministry of External Affairs. All of them were abroad.

Late at night, an old colleague, who was then working in another Ministry, rang me up in connection with something else. I explained my predicament to him. "If they want to do it," he said promptly, "they can do it in no time. l have got it done in the case of my own mother-in-law who had to go to the USA suddenly. They did it in 24 hours."

He explained to me how he had managed it. I did not want to follow the course he had adopted but asked him if I could quote the example of his mother-in-law to get my thing expedited. "By all means," he replied, "if that can help you."

Next morning, I was one of the first persons to barge into the room of the same IFS lady. She was surprised and said, "I have already pushed your case up, but I had asked you to come after a fortnight."

"Yes," I answered, "you had said so. Still I have come. And I have come to tell you that by no stretch of imagination I can be more dangerous than Mr so and so's mother-in-law.

She blushed profusely as I explained the lady's case to her and after mumbling a lot, asked me to meet her again the same evening. I met her, got my passport and managed to reach Kuala Lumpur in time for the course.

Moral: Other things being equal, nothing makes the Government work faster than precedents.

■■

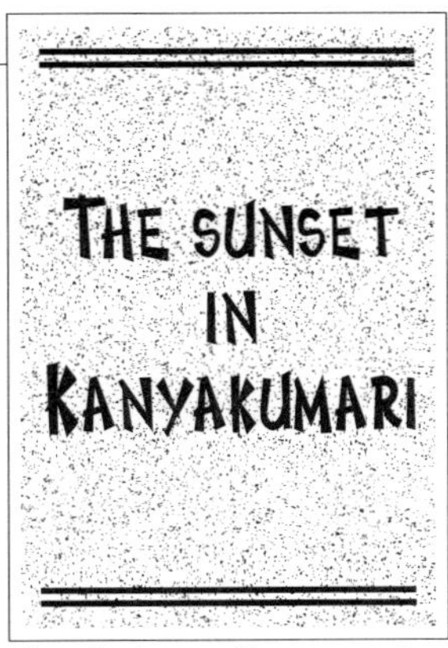

THE SUNSET IN KANYAKUMARI

Nowhere else in the world the sun sets as beautifully as in Kanyakumari. As it glides down gracefully in the horizon, it casts its golden spell on the bosom of the ocean below, making it rise and fall in gay abandon, and then, full of ecstasy, assuming various hues and shades, forms and shapes, recedes into the vast lap of the evening, leaving in its trail memories of moments no artist will ever be able to capture.

One wishes to breathe those sublime moments again and again. Life is what it is because of them and because of similar moments which nature makes available to man out of its infinite bounty. Of course, man cannot live without the other essentials like food, cloth and shelter. But then if these alone were to be the *sine qua non* of his existence, God might not have even created him.

Knowing my weaknesses, a close friend from Kerala, Gopakumar, took me all the way from Trivandrum to Kanyakumari during my last visit to his State. En route I wanted to stop for a while at Nagercoil in Tamil Nadu to see the house in which Kamraj used to live and to pay my homage to the memory of that giant among men who stood head and shoulders above his compatriots in the matter of practising what he preached – simple living and high thinking. I wanted to see the house and the wooden bench on which Kamraj used to sleep. I could see neither. Nagercoil that day was in the midst of a turmoil. Some political party had organised a big rally in support of some holy cause somewhere and this had blocked the traffic all round.

"The house is in a shambles," said Gopakumar, "what is there to see in it?" Yes, what was there to see in that house?

Bar mazar-e ma gariban, neh chirag-e, neh gule; neh par-e parvana sozad, neh sada-e bulbul-e (on my poor grave, there is no candle, no flower; no flutter of a moth, no song of a nightingale): I heard my own voice, thought of the magnificent memorials they have built for the great on the bank of the Yamuna in Delhi and wrang my hands in despair.

The sun was about to set in Kanyakumari. It had finished its foreplay with the ocean and was on the verge of taking its final dip into its mysteries before hiding itself in the darkness of the night. Sitting on the sands, as I watched this awe-inspiring spectacle of nature, my view was suddenly cut. A young couple, munching something, oblivious of the splendour so close, appeared from somewhere and stood between me and the sun.

The boy was wearing a black synthetic suit. Nothing could be more anachronistic. The girl was laden with gold. Apparently they were newly married. And apparently also they belonged to the neo-rich class. Their loud talk suggested this.

"All the way from Kapurthala," said the girl, "you have brought me here to show me what? Just sun and sand?"

"How did I know," retorted the boy, "that there will be nothing here except sun and sand? Those tourism fellows in Delhi were so much full of praise for this place. Anyhow don't you worry. Next year we will go to *vilayat*. That is a wonderful place, unlike what you see here."

■■

Take any ten women from the W.A.C.-(I) and ask them to form a straight line. They would fail to do so. That used to be the saying in 'World War-II when the W.A.C.-(I) – Women's Auxiliary Corps (India) – was first established in the Indian Army to shoulder the responsibilities of war, along with men.

The difficulty with those girls in *khaki* was that they were marvellously disproportionate in their structure. Some had too heavy bosoms and some had too heavy hips. Straighten the line from the front. The line behind would get further distorted. The British paid them well. And this aggravated the situation.

By and large, the W.A.C.-(I) panorama was shared by the rest of women in India. That no longer seems to be the case. In the matter of having a proportionate body, through slimming, the urban woman at least seems to have covered the distance of several generations in one.

Professions like modelling, acting in films and television, flying as air hostesses, public relations, advertising, business administration, sales promotion and even teaching have all contributed to this wonderful phenomenon. The craze for slimness indeed seems to be so overpowering that one hardly finds a modern home in Delhi which does not have a weighing machine.

In the kitchen there are all kinds of gadgets which obviate the need to squat on the floor. And on the roads, there is the sleek Maruti car. Whosoever designed this essentially feminine vehicle, he had, I suppose, the woman of today in mind.

The generation jump, which has hit the teenagers more than anyone else, has pushed the old *mataji-behnji* syndrome aside and yielded place to the new *yaar* society. In this society, everybody is everybody else's *yaar*. There is hardly any distinction between boys and girls. They dress alike, have the same hairstyles, use the same slangs and play the same games. They have their gangs and gang wars.

Of course, these wars are not like the gang wars of the underworld in Bombay (now Mumbai). These are decent and fought generally in the open, boys on one side and girls on the other, but not always so. Sometimes, the gangs are mixed – he's having a sprinkling of she's and vice versa. Whatever be their composition, they have one remarkable characteristic. In moments of crisis, like the one caused by the Mandal Commission, they join hands together.

And in moments of rejoicing, they have joint celebrations. I had the privilege of sharing one such moment with them on November 8, 1990.

It was the birthday party of a girl very dear to me. She had just completed her 13th year. Some 20 girls had collected together, one slimmer than another, all vivacious and full of life.

The elders, too, were there. But they were kept aside, like unaccompanied baggage.

The teenagers sang and danced merrily in dim light. The party went on till past midnight. At the end, there was the usual chorus song "many happy returns of the day," followed by what I had never heard before – "and lots of boyfriends on the way".

The girls clapped. The bewildered elders rubbed their eyes. They had cause to be grateful. For they managed to return home unmolested.

■■

"Someone big has died," said my wife, returning from the market, empty-handed, gasping for breath, "all shops closed. Nothing available, not even bread. Now make do with *besan-roti* (gram loaf), morning and evening."

But who was that big one? I asked her. That she didn't know. All she said was that he was too big. Never was the market closed so completely like that. She mentioned some names which I cannot mention and said at the same time, "Why don't they die together? And why should markets be closed when they die?"

I had no answer to that question. To get it, I switched on the TV – all the available channels of Doordarshan. Narasimah Rao was presiding over all of them, telling us, lesser mortals, how to be healthy and live longer. I switched on ZEE. There "mast-mast" was going on. Jain was showing some movie. ATN was doing the same. The local cable-wallah was advertising a house for sale.

With no mourning music on the TV, I went back to my newspapers. From top to bottom, I scanned every page of all the papers I get. There was no leader lying in precarious condition, nor anyone in coma. A number of Ministers were abroad. So were several committees surveying or studying how others placed in situations similar to ours are not committing mass suicides.

All those fellows would have been called back had someone died. No one knows when anyone dies. But politicians keep a watch on the situation. They are always wanting to know whose *gaddi* (seat) is likely to fall vacant. To get that *gaddi*, they sometimes even spread rumours that so and so is critically ill. There was no hint of even that in any newspaper.

However, I had to eat *besan-roti* in lunch. I did not want to do the same at night as well and so in the evening I went out to check who had died. None. All the markets were open, doing brisk business. The shopkeepers from whom I bought bread said to me, "In the morning, we had to close our shops, but that was just for ten minutes."

"Why?" I asked.

"Some woman leader," said he, "had been arrested somewhere. Her party workers here came and forced us to close our shops. We did so. But after they left, we reopened our shops. How the hell are we concerned who is arrested and where? They know their tricks. We know ours."

■■

I was going from Tara Apartments to the Medical Institute early one morning in July 1993 in a scooter-rickshaw (TSR). Suddenly I found, near Hauz Khas, the driver behaving in a strange manner. He gave violent jerks to the vehicle while it was still in motion.

What was he up to? For a while, I was reminded of those villains in films who run their cars at breakneck speed taking U-turns, L-turns, T-turns and all manner of other turns in order to dislodge the heroes or the police, grapling with them, out of their vehicles. Certainly, I was not that lucky.

Nor was I a soft target worthy of being robbed. Apart from my medical reports I did not have anything else in my hands. The watch I was wearing was not that expensive that it could tempt anyone to play foul with me.

Could it be that by jerking the rickshaw violently the fellow was trying to accelerate the meter? I looked at it but I could not read it. As the jerks continued, I remonstrated with him. He asked me to keep quiet. When I remonstrated with him a second time, he moved his vehicle to the left, slowed it down and stopped it close to the pavement.

"What has happened?" I said. "Nothing," he replied angrily "you'd better get down." I had no alternative but to get down.

"What is the matter?" I asked him, "I have to reach the Medical Institute before 9 a.m."

He pulled the rickshaw to the pavement, raised it upwards first from the front, then from the back, shook it left and right and threw it on its left side. He slapped it hard here and there, while giving it jerks simultaneously.

I thought something had gone wrong with the man. "Shall I take another rickshaw," I asked him. "No," he said lifting his vehicle back to its original position. "You'd better get in. We shall see what happens."

What could happen? I grew apprehensive. But I got back into the rickshaw. Short of turning it topsy-turvy, the man continued to wrestle with it till, to my great relief, we reached the Medical Institute.

He charged me no more than was reasonable. I was pleasantly surprised. As I made the payment, I asked him again. "What was the matter with your vehicle?"

"Nothing, sahib," he said "a rat had somehow infiltrated into the iron pipe that holds the canopy. It came out on the rubber piping above the screen and stared at me. It could have caused an accident. When I saw it, I shook the rickshaw. I shook it again and again to throw it off. But, alas it ran bock into the pipe and it is still there."

■■

According to my wife, my brain has gone out of order (*kharab ho gaya hae*). This discovery is not new. It is as old as our marriage. Like all other truths, it has to be stated again and again.

The latest provocation for the statement came one day last week when the two of us drove (together) into a huge building in Nehru Place which we had not seen before. "Looks very *aalishan* (magnificent)," said she. I agreed.

"Where are you going, *sahib*?" asked the liveried man there. He appeared to be like one of those great blokes you find at the entrance of five-star hotels. "I have to park the car," I said. "Do you have any work inside?" he asked. I looked at the building closely. It was the International Trade Centre, place for billionaires. My God, the ground slipped from under the wheels of the car.

"We have to park it just for ten minutes," said my wife, "only he has to buy a refill for his ballpoint pen". The man looked at her, smiled and said, "*Mataji*, the parking charges here are ten rupees per hour." "*Bera gharak* (boat is sunk)," whispered my wife. The man heard the remark, smiled again and chuckled, "*Chalo*, park it. We will see."

Now about the brain. My children and grandchildren know my weakness for ballpoints. One of them, Sumita, brought a Senator from somewhere and gifted it to me. The refill in it could not have lasted for ever. But when the time to replace it came, I found that it was not available in the local market. "Go to Nehru Place," said the stationery shop man, "there alone you will find the genuine stuff. They will charge you equivalent of a dollar or two."

The brain had to be declared out of order when the man in Nehru Place charged me Rs 65 for the refill. My wife frowned. But the man had already put the refill in the ballpoint. The die had been cast. Nothing could be done.

"*Betta*," said my wife to the liveried man, as we came out, "for a seven rupees worth of refill do we have to pay you ten rupees as parking charges?" The man looked at her yet again and chuckled yet again, "I had known that, *Mataji*, I have not even cut your *parchi* (car slip)."

I thanked him, put the car in the reverse gear and drove back home. I wanted to ask my wife why she had mentioned the price of the refill seven rupees, instead of sixty-five. But I didn't do so. For I have to live with her.

■■

'PEHLE AAP' TRAIN

There is nothing very strange about the goods train that some days ago ran past 13 railway stations and covered a distance of 94 km in two hours and 25 minutes without a driver. If the Americans can send their spacecraft into out space without an astronaut, why can't we run our trains without drivers? Science, after all, is nobody's monopoly.

Apparently the train was impatient. It could not put up with the *matlab* (purpose) of the driver and his assistant in getting down at the Matlabpur station on the Moradabad line of the Northern Railway. It waited for a while and then moved on. En route, the station masters must have shown it the red flag. Speeding at 60 kmph, it ignored all signals defiantly.

We must not forget that Moradabad, Matlabpur and the 13 stations which the train passed by are all in UP. There, anything can happen. Trains can move without drivers and trains with drivers can stay put where they are. I say this from personal experience. It happened years ago.

I was then the Press Attache to the Chief Minister of the State and was to accompany him to Naini Tal. We boarded the Kathgodam Express at the Charbagh railway station in Lucknow at about ten in the night. He went to his saloon and I took my reserved berth in a first class coupe. I was allowed to take a peon with me. Mathura Singh was the man. He was given a seat in the adjoining attendants' compartment and was to get me my tea early next morning at Haldwani, a little before Kathgodam, from where we were to move on to Naini Tal by road.

There was no other passenger in the coupe. Tired, I fell asleep quickly. But I remembered having heard the loud sound of the bugle of the engine and the shrill go-ahead whistle of the guard. I do not know how many stations the train passed by. But when I got up from my sleep in the morning, I found it was halting at one station. I took it to be Haldwani and looked for Mathura Singh. He was not there. I opened the door of the compartment and moved out. It was the Charbagh station in Lucknow.

I rushed towards the attendants' compartment. Mathura Singh, its solitary occupant, was snoring heavily. As I aroused him from his slumbers, he looked at me and said philosophically, "Sahib, go to sleep. We have not yet reached Haldwani."

"Where is the Chief Minister?" I asked him. "How can I tell?" replied Mathura Singh, "for all I know, he must also be sleeping in his saloon."

Later I learnt that the train was initially late by one hour, then by two hours. The Chief Minister cancelled his tour but the other passengers kept on sitting in their seats because there were "about to leave" announcements at regular intervals. Till morning the train had not moved at all.

Of course, the driver was very much there throughout. But apparently he was a strong believer in the "pehle aap" culture of Lucknow and was all along waiting for some other train to start first before he could move his own.

■■

I was returning from London. Two elderly Punjabi ladies were sitting in the twin seats ahead of me, "You live in London?" asked one of them. "No", said the other, "I had just come here to meet my *jatak* (son)."

Apparently they had not known each other before. But within a few minutes, they had exchanged so much information about their families that it occurred to me as if they were about to negotiate on matrimonial alliance between one's son and the other's daughter. Number of children, how many married, how many yet to be married, extent of property, husbands' occupation, names of aunts and uncles, fathers, grandfathers and their fathers and eventually the wonderful discovery that their great, greatgrandfathers were cousin brothers who had fought against the Moghuls under Maharaja Ranjit Singh – the two ladies were so much overjoyed that ignoring everyone else in the British Airways aeroplane, they almost rose in their seats arid embraced each other.

"How was your stay in London?" asked one.

"Very fine," said the other, "my *jatak* speaks English *phattaphat* (fluently). If someone hears him without seeing him, he will take him for an Englishman. His work is also very *vadiya* (good); repairs big, big cars in a garage.

"Englishmen are very lazy. They don't work on Saturday and Sunday. On these two days, cars come to his residence. He repairs them there and pounds come to him in showers. He is bathing in money."

"Someone should be there for his *dekhbhal* (to look after him)," suggested the one who had asked the question about the *jatak*, "why don't you stay on with him?"

"No, *behnji*, no", replied the *jatak*'s mother, "my son has all along been pressing me. But I will never stay there. There is none in London on whose forehead you don't find frowns. Particularly these *mems*. The moment they would see me, they gave me the feeling as if I had set them on fire."

She then narrated some incidents. "One morning", she said, "after taking my bath, l spread out the wet towel in the balcony for drying, No sooner had I done so than all the *mems* in the neighbourhood opened their own windows and started staring at me, as if I had taken away something from them."

"You should have also stared at them," said the other.

"I have done enough of staring," said the *jatak's* mother." I am not the one to lag behind. But what can I do if the *jatak* himself does not like my staring.

"He does not even allow me to put *mirch masala* in meat. When I came to London first, I found to my horror that he was taking boiled meat every day. I just could not eat it. Totally insipid. I wondered what had happened to him.

"Next day, I cooked the meat my own way, like we do in Punjab, put a lot of ghee and *mirch masala* in it and I am sure he liked it. But he said that I should not cook it that way in future."

"Why?"

"He says," said the *jatak*'s mother, "the flavour of rich *masala* travels to other houses and the Angrezi people do not like it. To hell with them, I said, I am off to Punjab: I cannot eat my food without *mirch masala*. And then I have to look after my own *gharwalla* (husband)."

■■

After a long time, I have received a secret envelope. It is from a national teaching-cum-research institute with which I have had the privilege of being associated for several years. The institute has to select candidates for the posts of Professor, Associate Professor and Reader for its communication department. I have been invited to serve on the selection board as an advisor.

Secret envelopes are dangerous. In the Government, they always contain something which, if revealed, can put your job in jeopardy. I do not know how many secrets lie buried deep down within me. Even after retirement, I cannot bring them out. I may not be hauled up. But my conscience will prick me. And I won't be able to stand that.

But there are two secret envelopes about which I can talk without running the risk of revealing any State secret. One belongs to my student days. It was glued to the inside cover of a book called *Hidayatnama Khavind* (Guide for Husbands). The book, written by a *kaviraj* who was also a B.A., was profusely advertised. The fact that it had a secret envelope inside was played up in particular.

I could not resist the temptation to buy the book. And even though I was in my teens, I read carefully what there was in the secret envelope. Broadly, it explained what to do and what not to do on the wedding night. There is no need to talk about that. For today's boys and girls know more about sex than what the kaviraj knew or thought it prudent to reveal.

The second secret envelope came my way much later, in the late seventies. I was living on the ground floor of a three-bedroom

Government flat. My next-door neighbour was a senior bureaucrat-cum-politician. He was closely related to a political high-up and his house was one of the hubs of political activities in that particular locality in New Delhi.

Almost every day, he used to receive baskets full of sweets or fruits or both from God knows where. My wife was envious. "You are holding an equivalent position in the Government", she would grumble, "why can't anyone send such baskets to you?"

Nobody did. But then one day, the gentleman moved on to a bigger AB-type bungalow not because he had been promoted but because the high-up to whom he was related rose further in the political hierarchy. Before leaving, he said to me, "someone will come from my hometown. He will bring something from my people. Kindly keep it with you. I will come in the evening and collect it from you. Kindly don't send him to my new house. He may lose his way."

That someone came and left a basket with my wife. She looked at it wistfully. Peeping from beneath the cluster of fruits and sweet boxes, which the basket contained, was a large, heavy, almost bulging secret envelope. What did it contain? Unto this day, I do not know.

■■

How many men in our cities can boast of knowing the art of stitching button on their shirt? Not many, I suppose, that is, of course, if we exclude those lost souls who are victims of self-inflicted bachelorhood and are condemned to live as such for the rest of their lives. In their struggle to keep their head above water, they manage to learn many things, including button-stitching which otherwise is essentially a feminine prerogative.

Male tailors have, no doubt, made some inroads into this situation. But they have done so less for the love of it than for the money it fetches them. By and large, for button-stitching, men are almost totally dependent on women, on their mothers as boys and on their wives as husbands. Women love this dependence. It helps them in strengthening their hold on men.

I must confess that I know nothing about the art of button-stitching. To the extent, that I can visualise it, the art involves five distinct operations: (a) selection of the right kind of button which means right colour, right holes, right dimensions; (b) selection of the right type of thread and needle; (c) putting the thread into the eye of the needle (how they do it, my God, I cannot imagine); (d) pushing the needle along with the thread into the most vulnerable hole; and (e) taking it out and repeating; (f) in all the other holes, one by one.

As if this is not enough, the mess created by the thread, because of its passage in and out of holes, has to be controlled and tightened in order that the button stays put where it ought to stay put. For this, the thread must go round its own neck a number of times. It is like the seven 'pheras' in a marriage ceremony.

Men being men, they take many things for granted in life. They become aware of the magnificence of the role that button-stitching plays so silently in strengthening their relation with their wives only when the latter run away. Mine did not run away. She just went to Calcutta (now Kolkata) to spend a couple of weeks with her younger brother, Kanwar, who had been inviting her for a long time.

Before leaving, she gave me detailed instructions about everything, from making ice in the freezer to boiling milk on the gas oven. But she made no mention of button-stitching. Apparently she thought that it was unnecessary or absolutely beyond me. But lo and behold, two days after she left, I found one of the buttons on one of my favourite shirts missing.

This particular shirt goes so well with the misty colour of the sky in the morning. I could not afford to leave it unused for two whole weeks. And so I took it to a tailor in the nearby market.

I was a little apprehensive that he might decline the job. But he did not. A jovial fellow, he managed to lay his hands on the right type of button and fixed it well. Of course, he charged a tidy sum for this.

As he handed the shirt back to me, he looked at my face with a twinkle in his eyes and asked, "how much did his shirt cost you?"

"I don't remember," I said, "but why do you want to know that?"

"Just by the way," the fellow blurted out, "the thing is that nobody wears this kind of shirt these days. It has been long out of fashion."

Button-stitching, I realised then and there, has more to it than meets the eye.

■■

From key-chains to T-shirts, almost everything seems to be available as a free gift in the market. The only condition is that it is tagged to something more expensive and that something we may not need or may not be able to afford.

And yet we feel tempted or provoked to buy it. The story of the big boost in the sale of potato chips of myriad varieties, which seem to have taken us by storm, bears testimony to what I am saying.

How did it start? With the free gift of stickers, the children went crazy. The more the stickers, the greater their sense of achievement. The parents had to yield. They knew that they could make the same chips at home at less than 20 per cent of the price they were paying for them. But they could not produce stickers. And the children were after stickers. Chips were incidental.

The current craze is to collect caps of bottles of certain brands of soft drinks. If you are able to lay your hands on the right cap, which has a prize sticker hidden below its inner lid, and you can know this only when you buy the bottle and open it, you may get anything – from free crates of the same drink to a Maruti car. Thirsty throats are getting thirstier. Prices mount up. We grumble about them. Yet the markets are flooded. And sales are jumping.

It is not an altogether new phenomenon. The old quiz in a certain magazine was perhaps the harbinger. It continues. But along with it have now come new kinds of puzzles asking you to fill a questionnaire and then to say why you consider a particular brand of tooth-paste or shaving cream to be the best. You may not be using the band advertised. You take to it because of the prize it offers. And this may be a free trip to Goa or Singapore for two.

I cannot forget my own experience of a free gift. I had it in Bangkok some ten years ago. As I walked into my room in the hotel where I stayed, a placard on the 'writing desk' greeted me. It proclaimed: "Welcome, you are our honoured guest. Come to Blue Heaven on the third floor for a delightful experience at our expense."

I had been to Bangkok earlier also. It was known to be a city of massage parlours. There were coffee houses within restaurants. These coffee houses were closed cabins where coffee was not the only thing that was served. And so I was a little chary. But since I was in Bangkok to attend a WHO seminar and WHO had made the stay arrangement, I took it that the hotel must be respectable and walked into its 'Blue Heaven'.

A beautiful Thai girl greeted me there. She conducted me to a table and gave me a list of drinks from which I could choose any. I opted for Vodka.

No sooner had I finished my first glass than she brought another one. When I said that one was enough for me, she pleaded that since she had already brought the second one, I should take it. I took it but at the same time said, "no more please."

As I finished my second glass, she came again and presented me with a bill for two pegs of Vodka. "But isn't it on the house?" I asked her. "Yes," she whispered, smiling mischievously, "provided you take four pegs. Less than that you have to pay for. That is the Blue Heaven rule."

I had to shell down a tidy sum. But since that day I have refrained from visiting any heaven, blue or black, which offers a delightful evening on the house or a free gift which is tagged to something which in normal circumstances may be beyond my reach or need.

■■

After retirement, most Government officers do not last long. Their wives do.

It is a matter of simple logic. With official accommodation taken away, telephone gone, supply of newspapers at Government expenses stopped, emoluments cut down to one-third or even less, officers just retired lose or gain weight faster than while in service. Either way, it is injurious to health which otherwise also is not expected to be that good at 58.

But more than anything else what hastens a retired Government officer's march to his ultimate destination is the loss of his authority. While in service, sitting in an air-conditioned room, he exercises almost absolute control over the destiny of numerous people. To underscore this position, he puts up a light outside his room. When this light turns red, take it that the bloke is seriously involved in something extremely important (it may even be a well-earned nap or a much needed chat or a cup of tea or coffee with a colleague) and, therefore, he must not be disturbed.

This authority whithers away the moment the officer is superannuated. Like a king forced to abdicate, he departs from the scene and recedes into wilderness wide which has no respect for what one might have been.

Wives of retired officers generally share with them all the vicissitudes of time. Except one. And that is loss of authority. Since in their husbands' heyday, they had none, they lose none. Their kingdom is their kitchen. And that they retain. The sun may or may not set over the British Empire. It cannot set over their supremacy in the kitchen.

During the last four years or so, I have lost half a dozen old acquaintances in the bureaucracy. Once upon a time, they used to be extremely busy – attending meetings, holding discussions with Ministers, handling Parliament questions, on tour in India or abroad. It was difficult to get them. But once they were superannuated, they knew not what to do with their time, were available easily and in the process fell down heavily in their own esteem.

Their widows continue to live. Not that they are happy. No widow can be. But they have their kitchen. The kitchen still belongs to them.

There is only one officer among those I was friendly with who, after retirement, lost his wife before he himself kicked the bucket. Earlier, he was always quarrelling with her. When she was gone, he did not know whom to quarrel with.

He went to Pondicherry in search of peace. There he stayed at Aurobindo's Ashram at Rs 30 a day. He came back soon for there was no peace in that heaven either. Besides, as he said, the price involved, including the cost of travel, was rather too much.

I wish God runs the world along new lines. There should be a *jeevan rekha* (lifeline), common to husband and wife. When the two of them reach this *rekha*, they should vanish together, leaving no trail behind.

When I try to share this thought with my wife, she becomes agitated. "You do what you like," says she, "I have a lot of work to do in the kitchen. There is no age of retirement there. It is my *jeevan rekha*."

■■

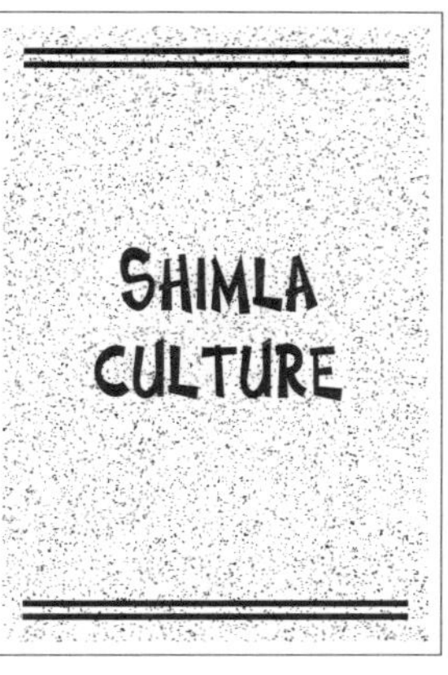

"You people who come from Delhi," said my journalist friend, long-based in Shimla, "think that everything happens over there and nothing happens anywhere else. Yes, everything happens in Delhi – intrigue, horse-trading, blackmail. I tell you that if someone were to drop a bomb on Delhi and wipe it off from the map of India, this country would be much better off. After all, Delhi has been destroyed several times. India lives."

"So does Delhi," I might have said, but I didn't. I had provoked him unnecessarily through an indiscreet remark, "what do you people do here in winter?"

We were sitting in a restaurant – some members of the Press corps and a couple of officials. For nearly a month I had been in the town. Nothing had happened – I mean, nothing of the type that happens in Delhi daily, during the entire period which the Press could write back home about.

There had been no incident of anyone knocking at the door of a house-wife, whose husband might have been away, and robbing her of her valuables after pushing her into the bathroom and bolting the door from outside. Nor of any old couple living alone in a corner flat being stangulated to death by their long-trusted servant. No bomb blasts, no attacks by terrorists, no warnings by the police asking the people to report the presence of suspicious-looking characters to them or not to touch objects abandoned on the roads or hidden in the bushes.

It was indeed heart-warming to see young girls roaming about alone and freely on the Mall and the side-walks late in the evening without any fear of molestation. No eve-teasing, no snatching of purses, no kidnapping. I tried to locate at least one advertisement on abortion on the walls, I did not find any.

If that is the situation during the peak summer season, what can happen in the town when winter comes and the bazaars are deserted? That was what I had in mind when I threw up that silly question. I explained all this to my journalist friend and further mollified his feelings by telling him that long time back, when I used to be with *The Pioneer* of Lucknow, the only story we would receive in winter from our correspondent in Naini Tal was about someone having been mauled by a tiger. The joke in the paper was that he had kept cyclostyled copies of the story with him and filed them year after year.

"Things do happen in Shimla in winter also," the gentleman explained, "it is the Capital of a State. We have a State Assembly. Recently there were elections to the Lok Sabha. Nothing untoward happened because the people here are more civilised. They are not like Delhiites who are a law upto themselves."

As I left the restaurant and drifted on the Mall, carefree and alone, suddenly I found myself involved in a head-on collision with a buxom lady coming from the opposite direction. She almost fell down on the road.

"I am extremely sorry," I apologised to her, "I did not see you."

"That is all right," she said understandingly, and then, straightening herself up and surveying me from head to foot, added in a somewhat stern voice, "but you are walking on the wrong side of the road. See that."

She pointed towards a small plaque set in the retention wall opposite. It said, "Please keep to the left."

■■

"Where is my ceiling fan?" asked the Jhuggi Jhonpri Man (JJM). "I had promised it to you," said the man with the beard, "but first you get your electricity." "And where is electricity?" asked the JJM. "That was not my promise," said the man with the beard, "that was the promise of the man without any hair on his head".

JJM went to the man without any hair on his head. "I agree that I had promised you that you would get your electricity," said the latter, "but first your colony has to be approved." Why not have it approved then?" asked JJM. "That was not my promise," said the man without any hair on his head, "that was the promise of the man with the white cap on his head."

JJM went to the man with the white cap on his head. "I stand by my promise," said the latter "and I shall get your colony approved in no time. But the land on which it has been set up has first to be acquired from those to whom it belongs." "Why not have it acquired then?" asked JJM. "That was not my promise," said the man with the white cap, "that was the promise of the man who wears a safari suit."

JJM went to the man who wears a safari suit. He was not there. He had gone to the Raj Bhavan to attend a meeting. "What do I do then?" asked JJM. "You leave your address here," said MOMSS (the man in the office of the man in the safari suit), "I will send you a letter giving the date and time of your appointment."

"But I have no address," said JJM. "Where do you live then?" asked MOMSS. "I live in a *kachcha* colony behind the road," said JJM. "What is the name of the road?" asked MOMSS. "I don't know," said JJM, "the *thekedar* (contractor) knows. I am only building the road. I don't know its name. I work on *dehari* (daily wage) basis."

"But the road must be having some name?" asked MOMSS. "Sahib," said JJM.

"How do I know? I come from a village. We have no roads there."

"In that case," said MOMSS, "you better come again."

"Will I get my pension also?" asked JJM, "that pension?" said MOMSS. "Netaji had promised," said JJM. "That our jobs would become permanent and we all would get pension."

"You better come again," said MOMSS. "When should I come?" asked JJM. "Come when Netaji comes," said MOMSS.

■■

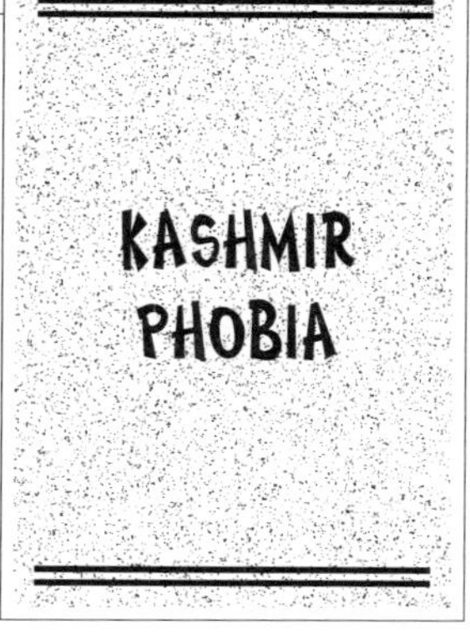

KASHMIR PHOBIA

"What exactly is your trouble?" asked hakim sahib. "I am having pain," said the patient.

"In which part of your body?" asked the hakim.

"I do not know," replied the patient. "Sometimes it is here and sometimes there and sometimes it is all over. It travels from one part of my body to another. So much so that it makes me forget which part of my body is what.

"Sometimes I feel that my hands are my feet and even start walking on them. Sometimes it is the other way round, and I start eating with my feet. I am in an awful mess, why even my eyes remain tightly shut. Whatever I see, I see through my ears and through my nose."

"Lie down," said the hakim. And the patient fell flat on the ground. He was hefty and apparently in the pink of health. The hakim was the famous *hakim-e-azam* and carried the formidable degree of HUHMTJ, which meant *hazik-ul-hukma, mahar-e-tib-o-jarat,* which, translated into simple English, means great among physicians, expert in medicine and surgery.

The hakim examined the patient thoroughly, felt his pulse, and then asked: "How is your *hazma* (digestion)?"

I feel hungry all the time," said the patient.

"How many meals do you have in a day?" asked the hakim.

"Five," said the patient, "morning tea, breakfast, lunch, evening tea, and then supper." "Did you take anything to eat with your tea this morning?", the hakim asked.

"Yes."

"What was it?" asked the hakim.

"Kashmir," the patient replied.

"What did you have as breakfast?" queried the hakim.

"Kashmir," said the patient.

"And in your lunch?" asked the hakim.

"Kashmir," replied the patient again.

"And with tea in the evening?" asked the hakim.

"Kashmir," again repeated the patient.

"And in dinner?" asked the hakim.

"Kashmir," was the reply.

"Did you take anything between meals?" asked the hakim.

"Yes," replied the patient.

"What was it?" asked the hakim.

"Kashmir."

"Go into the bathroom and take off your clothes," said the hakim. "I have to examine you further." The patient dutifully followed the hakim's instructions.

Inside the bathroom, the hakim knocked at the patient's chest and stomach, and then bent his arms and legs up and down, but he found nothing wrong with them. Then he twisted his head to the left and then to the right.

"It pains," gasped the patient.

"Never mind," said the hakim, "I have to examine the condition of your brain."

At the end of the detailed examination, the hakim gave the following prescription to the patient:

Name of patient – Pakistan.

Disease – Kashmir phobia.

Medicines – None.

Precautions – Stop eating Kashmir.

■■

I was inside a Government dispensary waiting for my medicines which the storekeeper was trying to locate in the wooden boxes lying by his side, when suddenly the lights went off. He lighted a couple of matchsticks. That did not help.

"Don't you have a candle?" I asked him. "No," he said, "the government does not supply candles." I suggested that if he had no objection, I might get one for him from the shop opposite. He had no objection.

The shopkeeper from the opposite shop took out a candle from a bundle but when I offered him a ten-rupee note, he became peevish. "Don't you have a rupee?" he asked angrily. "No," I said. "Early morning," shouted he, "is the time for my *boni* (first sale), and here you come asking me to part with nine rupees."

"But I am only buying a candle from you and I am paying for that," I said to him politely, to which he retorted in the same angry tone, "no change, no candle, *ghar ka rasta dekho* (take the road to your house)."

I was surprised. It occurred to me that the shopkeeper either had a bad liver or he had a quarrel with his wife. The shop was a part of his house – unauthorised, I believe. But that was none of my business.

I looked around for my wife. She had accompanied me in the car but disappeared the moment we reached the dispensary and she spotted a *rehriwalla* selling apples. It is her firm belief that the apples which the *rehriwallas* sell in DDA colonies are cheaper and fresher than what are available in our locality. I managed to spot her and asked if she had a one-rupee coin. She didn't have it, but then she took over the responsibility from me.

I kept away – outside the range of anything the angry shopkeeper might feel provoked to throw at me. Within a few minutes, my wife returned to where I was and handed me a candle. "How did you manage it?" I asked her, quite taken aback.

"I bought the whole bundle of ten candles from him," said she triumphantly, "and in the process I have saved five rupees as well. In our market, those bloody sharks charge fifteen rupees for a bundle. This man charged only ten rupees. This place is cheaper. I have always told you so."

"What about the cost of petrol?" I might have asked her. But I didn't. I could only say, *aurton ka jawab nahin* (none like women), just as Kapil Dev says in that famous shaving cream ad, *Palmolive da jawab nahin.*

The moral of the story is that as and when you go to government dispensary next, carry a candle or a one-rupee coin with you.

■■

There used to be a clerk in the Estates Department of the UP Government who would be present at the Charbagh railway station in Lucknow every time an important member of the Cabinet boarded the train from there. He would lay the bed for the dignitary in his coach. When he did it for the first time, he was hauled up by the shadow of the Minister concerned and handed over to the nearby police station where his identity was soon established and he wad released on tendering an apology.

He resumed his activity the very next day. Gradually the personal staff of Ministers learnt to put up with him – and also to welcome him. They thought, perhaps, that he had received some specialised training in France or somewhere else in the art of laying beds for the gentry. For nobody laid beds in rail-coaches better than he did. He became a familiar figure at the Charbagh railway station, and from the station superintendent to Ghasi Ram, the porter, everybody started calling him "bedding adviser" to honourable Ministers.

How was the man able to lay his hands on the tour programmes of Ministers, which are supposed to be confidential? Well, till 1960, when I left Lucknow, that was a mystery. But much later I learnt in Delhi that he had gone up step-by-step and become a big shot in the Estates Department.

I never got an opportunity to meet the gentleman and there was no reason why I should think of him at all. But then, one day, recently, as I read in the newspapers about the arrest of a certain shoe thief in Delhi, I found the bed adviser's indefinable face suddenly emerging from somewhere and laughing at all and sundry.

The shoe thief, Siddarth, alias Mohammad, 30, so said the story, used to read the obituary columns of newspapers as a source of his own livelihood. These columns would reveal to him the venue of meetings announced to condole the death of not ministers but people otherwise important. He would go to these venues and from there quietly take away the shoes of the mourners. Obviously he was choosy in selecting his shoes. For the story also said that he took the shoes all the way to Bombay (now Mumbai), his hometown and sold them there. The enterprise fetched him as much as Rs 10,000 every month.

The man was caught red-handed in a mosque in the Chandni Mahal area of the Capital. When the police searched his room in the posh guest house in which he was staying, they recovered from his possession 31 brand new pairs of shoes.

"Luck does not favour all," I can almost hear the bed adviser telling the shoe thief teasingly.

■■

"Move away, move away, clear the way," two persons, then three, then four shouted and everybody around ran helter-skelter, jumping on to the pavement. I did not know what was happening and kept walking on my side of the road. I looked at it. It was as dirty as it had always been. That made it obvious that no VIP was coming. Had some been coming, the road, which leads to the Tughlaqabad shooting range on the outskirts of Delhi, would have definitely worn a better look. It would have been cleaned the precious night and dressed up again in the morning. The parapets would have been white-washed. No such thing had happened.

No VIP. Then what? Some terrorists? No sign of them either. Nor of any policeman. Had there been some terrorists, a patrol van would have come from somewhere at least to find out where they had gone. And there would have been some panic in the area. No such thing. Probably someone had picked someone's pocket and the people had caught him and were dragging him to the police post. I did not see any sign of that also. Could be there was an accident. And not knowing what to do, everybody was asking everybody else to clear the way for the victim to be taken to the hospital. Nobody was taking anybody. There was no victim. There was no accident.

Within the twinkling of an eye, a tall, hefty fellow in *kurta-pyjama*, with a shawl thrown on his shoulders, pushed me aside and threw me down on the pavement. Naturally I was furious. The pavement was full of potholes and pitfalls, with human waste and cowdung scattered all over it. I managed with great difficulty to save my clothes, as well as my body, stood up and asked the man angrily why he had done that kind of thing to me.

"Have you lost your mind?" he darted back at me, "didn't you see everybody else getting away from the road? Had I not pushed you on to the pavement, the cow would have killed you. She would have pierced her sharp horns into your frail body and left you bleeding here on the road."

Bewildered, I stared at the fellow and asked him what exactly had happened. Apparently a Gujjar, he explained to me condescendingly that one of the men asking people to get off the road was carrying a new-born calf in his arms and the calf's mother, the cow, was on her heels, providing a protective cover to her babe. She would have knocked down anybody crossing her path.

I had thought that that kind of privilege belonged to VIPs alone. It is dangerous to cross their path; I mean to come between their bullet-proof limousines and the commando cars that escort them. But I did not know that it was equally dangerous to cross the path of a cow shadowing her calf. I thanked my benefactor and walked back home.

■■

In Kipling's old paper, 'The Pioneer' of Lucknow, which I had the privilege to serve long ago, we used to have a lovely, little News Editor who had a lovely, little motor car. Even though Lucknow in those days was a town of lotus-eaters, where nobody could be accused of doing anything of consequence, we had to keep the paper going, for on that depended our livelihood.

As part of our struggle for survival, every night we, the reporters and the sub-editors, had to caress, cajole and coerce the little car of our little News Editor in order to make it move homeward. A Baby Austin of yore, made in England, living much beyond the years of its life expectancy, it was indeed a remarkable specimen of the glory that once was Britannia.

Parked in the midst of our two-wheelers, it announced its presence at once, being, to quote Tennyson, the "roof and crown of things". It was hard to make it move. But once it moved, it moved on gracefully, in the manner of some coquettish courtesan of Oudh, entertaining an admiring Nawab in the latter's '*ishrat kadda*' (pleasure resort) far from the madding crowd.

The car had a maximum speed of ten miles per hour. Whenever our little News Editor was late, and he was late more often than not, we used to think that his little car had been run over by a pedestrian loitering in the fashionable bazaar of Hazratganj close to the Secretariat and the Assembly building.

Almost half a century has gone by since I last saw that wonderful car. It is a measure of the progress journalism has made during this period that reporters and sub-editors have no longer to push the cars of their News Editors at night. Of course, not all

News Editors own cars. Thanks to their value-based attachment to the thing called freedom of the Press, the automobile explosion seems to have left most of them unscathed.

Once in a month I have to meet the Editor of the Hindustan Times paper. Earlier, the American Library, which is almost next-door to the Hindustan Times House and of which I am a member, used to give shelter to my car. For understandable security reasons, they have stopped this facility.

In the Hindustan Times House itself, the 'Parking Full' board almost always stares you in the face. Outside, on Kasturba Gandhi Marg, no parking is permitted by the police.

Where to park the car? That is a big problem whenever I go to Kasturba Gandhi Marg to meet my Editor or to pick up a couple of books from the American Library. Last month, having no other alternative, I left it on the road itself and asked my wife to keep sitting in it. That was to suggest that the halt there was absolutely brief and purely incidental or accidental and, as such, not a cognizable offence. But my meeting with the Editor lasted a bit longer. And when I returned, I found my wife involved in a heated exchange of words with two police cops.

They wanted her to get down from the car in order that it should be towed away. She was insisting that if it was to be towed away, it should be towed away along with her, sitting in the car. That cruelty they did not seem prepared to inflict on the lady. Maybe they thought it was not a good thing to do particularly in the year of the girl child!

I apologised to the cops from the core of my heart and they were gracious enough to let us go.

On the way back home, as my wife kept on harping on my indiscretion, I thought of the lovely little car of our lovely little News Editor. Weren't those better days? To give a little push to a little car does entail some exertion. But in the process you don't have to part with your wife. Or to face the music from the police.

If the Editor had detained me a bit longer, I might have come back home sans my wife sans my car! ■■

During my long stint in the ministry of health and family welfare in the 70s, I had a remarkable organisation called MMU (mass mailing unit) under me. It had three principal components – a large printing press, a library of addresses of nearly a million leaders of public opinion in the country and a sizable distribution wing. The total strength of the staff approximated 200.

The organisation was born in the early 50s when the family planning revolution swept India. And like many other things that came in those days, it was a gift from America under the USAID programme. The US took some of the key personnel of the outfit for training round the world. It also supplied paper for all that the press was to produce.

The idea was great. Print inhouse all that you need. All that you want your people to read. And distribute it from one point, New Delhi, so that you can have total control over the situation.

Nearly one hundred categories of people who could sail under the banner of opinion leaders – from ministers to panchayat leaders – were identified. There was a scientific system to update their addresses continuously. For instance, when Morarji Desai replaced Indira Gandhi in New Delhi, all that was to go to the Prime Minister went to him and not to Mrs Gandhi.

But what was it that went to Mrs Gandhi or to Morarji Bhai? Or, for that matter, to the numerous other categories of dignitaries known as leaders of public opinion? That big link in the system was missing. I was told that the earlier intention was to appoint writers in all the principal Indian languages and to make them write all that was needed to be conveyed to the recipients. Those writers were to write folders, pamphlets, leaflets and things like that. The press was to print them. And the distribution wing was to take care of disbursement.

Writers, though available cheaper by the dozen then as now, could not be appointed. Some ban came in their way. So, while there were no writers to write what was to be written, a large battalion of artists, draughtsmen, copyholders, paste-up boys and blokes like that emerged on the scene. They were to give artistic shape to what the writers were to write. But since writers were not there and since the press had to justify its existence, it produced calendars and New Year greeting cards that went from top bosses in the ministry to all concerned, including those in Bollywood and Hollywood.

Well, it is a free country and everybody here is entitled to do what he wants to do with what he gets. If they can do it in Parliament, why not elsewhere?

That, however, was not my principal concern. My principal concern was how to stop the theft of lead and expensive paper from the press and what work to assign to those in position in what was known as their 'spare time'.

In the ministry of finance, they have an organisation called SIU (staff inspection unit). Turn by turn, it studies ministries to locate surplus posts. When it came to the health ministry, it picked up MMU and recommended its abolition. I supported the recommendation whole-heartedly. But MMU could not be abolished.

For, the prevalent practice then, as now, was that talent once established in the government must not be done away with. Second, and more pertinent in today's context, people likely to be affected if they are asked to go can legitimately put it to the finance minister. If you can have nearly 100 ministers in UP and another 100 in Bihar and they can spend crores of rupees on tea and snacks alone, why deprive us of our little morsels of bread?

■■

Early in the morning, in the city forest a young girl wearing a devastating T-shirt passes by me. The shirt carries but one word – Kellog. Apparently the girl has got it as a prize in some competition. Clever of the people behind the corn flakes carrying that brand name. The girl proclaims the brand more loudly than any ad could possibly do.

How many such shirts the people responsible for the campaign must have distributed to boys and girls? How many mobile models have they thus made available for themselves for a song? If one books a bit of wall space for an ad, one has to pay heavily for it. For a hoarding, the amount can be several times more.

The T-shirt in the circumstances is the cheapest medium. Other things apart, it gives to the medium, the one who uses it, an enormous sense of achievement.

That is not the case with the girl who rings me up later during the day to enquire whether I have got an inverter at home. She is a bit disappointed when she gets my answer in the affirmative. But not to be defeated, she puts to me another question quickly, "Do you have a chappati-maker?" I tell her that I don't eat chappaties. She bangs the phone.

I am allergic to TV. But I do watch the Indian cricket team being smashed to bits by anyone and everyone, where it goes. And I also watch the news-bulletins put across by STAR and BBC. Everything I see on TV screen is interspersed with swashbuckling boys and girls, clad or semi-clad, according to the demands of various situations, selling all kinds of new goods.

Hema Malini stretches forth her hands and says, "*Mein to tung aa gai hoo* (I am fed up)." Rightly so. The soap with which she has been washing her clothes has let her down. Her hands have gone dry and developed cracks. Calls for national mourning, I whisper to myself. But then someone appears on the scene and shows us a new soap which is an answer to Hema's problems.

The latest trend is they are getting hold of housewives who tell us as housewives alone can tell us why they use this or that in preference to this or that. A young girl comes in to whisper, "Mummy, I want to be a queen." The next moment we see her being crowned as a queen – thanks to a particular shampoo.

If Juhi Chawla can sell Lux, why not Sridevi? And if Azhar can sell shoes, what is wrong with Tendulkar selling Pepsi? Mercifully, no politician has so far been brought forth to prescribe for us a recipe for various kinds of scams and scandals.

"Don't you think this is needed?" I ask an ad professional, one of the tallest in India. He smiles at me and says, "Not until they pay me 35 per cent of the total they get."

I am at his residence near Malabar Hill in Mumbai. "When are you coming to Delhi?" I ask him, seriously meaning to invite him to my place, in reciprocation. He gives me the dates and I want to know from him where he will stay in Delhi. "With my wife, of course," is his instant reply, "we have perfect understanding.

I am a bit surprised, for he and his wife have long been divorced. The perfect understanding, I figure out, is that when she goes to Mumbai, she stays with him and when he goes to Delhi, he stays with her.

That is the adman's world – everything "perfect". Natural, I suppose.

■■

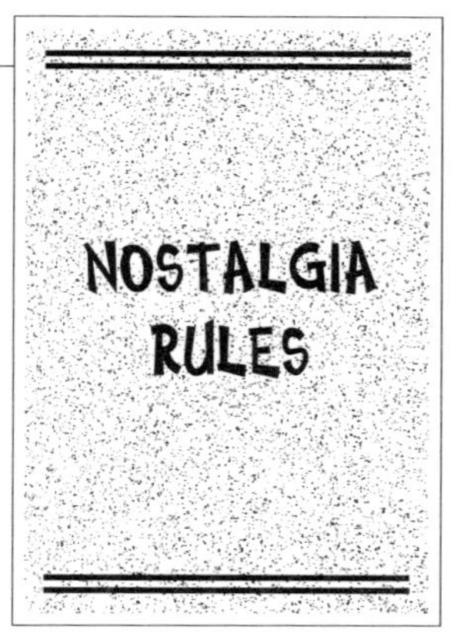

Outside their own countries, wherever Indians and Pakistanis meet – particularly those belonging to the fading generation that crossed the border – they introduce themselves and start a "dialogue". It does not take time to become informal and go back to the ages left behind: to roam about in towns and villages, lost but not forgotten, and to talk about people who once used to be your neighbours.

Whenever I meet anyone from Peshawar, the town to which I once belonged, nostalgia overtakes me completely and I ask the stranger questions about my old alma mater, Islamic College, about my own locality, Mohalla Kakaran and all that I can recall.

Any mention of a familiar person, family or shop from the other person is enough to bring me to the edge of my chair – if I am seated, that is. Rapport strengthens. No politics come in the way. No talk about Kashmir. I have indeed never heard any such talk in any of my encounters with people from Pakistan in the course of my visits abroad.

One such occasion was when I participated in a UN workshop on grassroot communication in Kandy, Sri Lanka. Some 20 people, from 10-12 countries, had come to attend the workshop. We were taken to the spot in a luxury bus – courtesy Sri Lanka Broadcasting Corporation.

Latif, a TV producer from Peshawar and posted at Islamabad, was sitting by my side. We began talking in Hindko, a mixture of Punjabi and Pushtu. It was exhilarating to come across someone who can talk to you in that language. Certainly our conversation had nothing to do with the subject of the workshop.

A Sri Lankan, sitting close by, saw us thus engrossed and was suddenly overtaken. "One thing highly objectionable about you Indians," he said, "is that whenever you meet, you altogether forget that others, too, are sitting with you." Both of us looked in his direction, slightly amused. He continued, "How would you feel if we Sinhalese, too, started talking in our own language?" Latif corrected him to say that he was not from India but from Pakistan and I mentioned that while originally I was from Pakistan, after Partition, I had settled in Delhi.

Nevertheless, we apologised to him for our indiscretion and all was well thereafter. On a long stretch of the road to Kandy, there is a cashewnut bazaar, where young Sinhalese women sell cashewnuts wrapped in long belt-like strips of plastic cloth, made secure against heat, dust and moisture.

Ranjit Tilakratne, our Sinhalese friend, helped us in buying those cashewnuts, singing a thousand songs in their praise. "Locally grown, roasted at home by mothers and grandmothers, such cashewnuts are available nowhere else in the world. You can keep them for months and they still remain fresh," he told us. Impressed more by his salesmanship than the nuts, we bought several strips.

During the stay, we were lavishly entertained by our Sri Lankan hosts. Most of us developed a warm relationship between ourselves. I got to know a lot about their family, workplace and problems and vice versa. Among the many get-togethers that were arranged, the one which left a permanent mark on my mind was at the residence of Ranjit, at the outskirts of Colombo.

As the drinks were poured and the party gathered our Sinhalese friend requested his wife to sing us a song. Lo and behold, she sang one of the popular old Hindi film songs: *Aey chand chhup na jaana, jab tak mein geet gaoon....* (Hide not, oh moon, as long as I sing my song; this tune of life, as long as I play it to my heart's content).

Neither Ranjit nor his wife knew either Hindi or Urdu. But they knew their music.

■■

MEETING GROUND

When a woman prime minister in Pakistan eases to be in office, her husband is pushed into jail. In India whenever a male chief minister ceases to be in power, his wife takes over from him as chief minister.

There is so much in common in the tale of the two countries that I fail to understand what the dickens it was that separated them. What Inzamam-ul-Haq did recently in Toronto, rushing with an uplifted bat towards a spectator who was calling him potato repeatedly, Lala Amarnath had done long, long ago in Lucknow.

A match between India and Pakistan was going on. One youth from the audience was heckling a Pakistani fielder. Lala Amarnath was batting – or maybe he was waiting for his turn to bat. He charged towards the heckler and might have hit him but the latter ran away. All was quiet thereafter.

In the lobby of a hotel in Bangkok, I once found three young men sitting in easy chairs, removing morsels of meat stuck in the cavities of their teeth with sharp toothpicks. They were wearing the kind of dress I used to wear in my hometown, Peshawar, and were speaking a language I used to speak over there, Hindko.

"Anyone amongst you from Peshawar?" I threw the sentence at them in the manner of one on familiar ground. All three were from there. And all three insisted that I should join them.

They took me to their room which they were sharing. And there they made me eat *pista-badam* which they had brought from home. In Peshawar, any time used to be tea-time. Not in Bangkok. But then, people from India and Pakistan don't believe in doing in Rome as Romans do. They believe in doing what they themselves do back home.

One of the three took charge of preparing tea in the typical Peshawar fashion. He poured milk and sugar in the pot and stirred the concoction furiously with a spoon. He took one spoonful of it from the tea-pot and sipped it. Apparently it was not sweet enough. He put a bit more of sugar and stirred the concoction in the same manner. He tasted the tea with the same spoon again.

Finally, when the tea came up to his desired taste, he pronounced *tiarsho* (it is ready), poured it in cups and we all drank it. That was the way it used to be done in Peshawar.

Not that there was any shortage of spoons over there. The important thing was that the tea must not let the host down. Secondly, in situations such as the one in Bangkok, the spoon silently served as some sort of symbol of sharing.

We discussed numerous things. But neither politics nor Kashmir. They were traders and least concerned about either. I do not know whether they knew who the governor of their own province was. They were more interested in knowing the price of wheat, rice and sugar in Delhi. And equally interested they were in knowing the price of clothes, watches and umbrellas.

"Tell me one thing," one of them asked me, as I was about to take leave from them, "Is it the same in India?"

What was what? I naturally enquired. "In Pakistan," replied the man, and he seemed to be a bit better educated, "for everything, we always have to pay something to those bloody government officers. We pay them to get our visas. When we go back home with the goods that we buy here, we pay them bumper sums to get them cleared at the customs. If we don't grease their palms, our trade comes to naught. Tell me frankly, in the name of God, is it the same in India?"

What could I reply to that?

■■

A sad occasion took me to the cremation ground on Lodhi Road in the second half of January 1993. The last time I had visited that place was nearly a decade ago. During the interval, it has undergone some changes: I noticed three in particular.

Almost every five minutes, and I stayed there for an hour or so, a corpse was brought in. There was a pell-mell kind of situation. Mourners accompanying one dead body were getting mixed up with those accompanying another. Some foreign visitor watching the scene might have come to the conclusion that some awful disease had broken out in Delhi.

The number of platforms on which they burn the dead had gone up appreciably. Yet, almost every platform or pit was occupied. These had numerical markings. I was told that advance booking for either (pit or platform that is) had to be made before a corpse could be brought there.

What happens if there is no booking? The occasion was such as did not permit me to raise this question up with anyone. But I thought of Singapore.

There they are digging up old graves to accommodate the newly dead. Maybe in India, just as we take two or more patients on one single bed in a hospital, we start burning several dead bodies together at one particular spot. That certainly would be economical, what with the 'cost' of death being what it is!

We are a genuine people. Our culture has deep and varied roots and finds manifestation at all places.

This is the second point which struck me. I could not count the number of cement or marble benches on the ground. But I saw them all, one by one, and read the words written on them:

"In memory of so and so, son of so and so, who left for his heavenly abode on such and such date – donated by his son or daughter or wife, so and so." All over I came across such moving words. They touched the core of my heart. And I felt proud of the *family traditions* we continue to cherish.

But the third thing which I saw almost drove me around the bend. In one corner of the cremation ground, there is a large wash-basin, made of cement, with a good number of taps on it. As I was washing my hands there, I could not help noticing the sticker on the wall behind it. It said in Hindi: "In Kashmir, many a temple was demolished; but no tear was shed by any eye."

A number of people were washing their hands along with me. "Couldn't they think of some other place for it?" I asked one. He shrugged his shoulders contemptuously, took out a hanky from his pocket, dried his hands with it and walked away.

■■

I was sitting in the room of the babus in the Municipal Committee office in Peshawar. It was in February, 1939. I had gone to that office for the registration of my grandfather's death. The babus had just started settling down to work. They had finished their *kawa* (green tea) and were rubbing their hands to warm them up. Suddenly an elderly Pathan walked into the babus' room and announced, "Hazoor, Habibullah's wife has given birth to a boy".

"When was it," asked one of the babus, "and how?"

"Last night, hazoor," said the man, "Habibullah's father came this morning and informed me."

"But how can that happen?" said the babu, "last night it was raining heavily?"

"It was raining heavily, no doubt," submitted the man, guiltily, "but the baby was born. That is what Habibullah's father has told me."

Mischievously, the babu looked at the man, surveyed him from head to foot and then put it to him: "As the mohalladar of your mohalla, don't you know that under the orders of Hakumat-e-Britannia, no baby can be born in rain?"

"Khuda ki kasam, hazoor?" asked the man in all innocence.

"Khuda ki kasam," said the babu, "if as the mohalladar of your mohalla, you don't know even this, then what kind of a mohalladar are you?"

Perplexed, the man said: "God is my witness. I have committed no sin. I am a law-abiding citizen. And if this is the *farman* (order) of Hakumat-e-Britannia that babies should not be born in rain, I will go back to my mohalla and ask Habibullah to find out how his wife has violated the *farman*."

"Yes," said the babu, "go back at once and make enquiries, if your life is precious to you, and then come to me again and let me know how this has happened. Thousands of *khurafats* (nonsensical things) are happening in Peshawar, but this kind of a thing has never happened. In my long service of 15 years in the municipality, I have never come across a single case of a baby having been born in rain. For all that takes place anywhere, I mean, all that I have to record in any registers, I am answerable to the sarkar and the sarkar is no bloody fool that it has appointed me to this post. I am holding a responsible position. One wrong entry in any of my registers, and the *hakim* (officer) above me will chop off my head".

The mohalladar touched his ears and murmured: "*Toaba, toaba, Khuda aisa na kare* (mercy, mercy, may God not do that!) Have faith in Him. He who has none else, He is with him."

So saying, the mohalladar dashed off to find out how against the *farman* of Hakumat-e-Britannia, Habibullah's wife had given birth to a baby in rain. I can't say what happened thereafter. But I am reminded of that hilarious episode from my days in Peshawar as I read in the newspapers all this *khurafat* about the pregnancy of Cherie Blair, wife of Tony Blair, Prime Minister of Britain.

How can a Prime Minister spare time to make love to his wife in the midst of heavy demands on him as PM? This they are debating.

Well, may I say, if a baby can be born to a man's wife on a rainy night in Peshawar against the orders of the British Government, why can't Her Majesty's most obedient servant make love to his wife while serving Britain as its Prime Minister?

■■

Better to Lose Your Life than Your Wife

"Sada suhagwati raven* (may your husband always remain alive)" – that is what the girl's mother tells her daughter blessedly as the girl leaves her *maika* for her *sasural*. In earlier times, the mother also used to say "*satputri hoven* (may you have seven sons)". That second blessing is no longer showered. Apparently, boys, if they come cheaper by the dozen, are, like everything else, subject to the laws of diminishing returns.

What is it that girls and their mothers don't do for the long life of hubbies? The festival of *karvachauth* is celebrated throughout Punjab, as well as elsewhere in Northern India, with downright solemnity. On that day, married women don't eat anything. Late in the evening, dressed like brides, with thalis containing sweets, flowers, lighted little lamps and all that in hand, they perform their community husband puja. They break the fast at night only when they sight the moon. Sometimes, the moon does not oblige because of clouds. In such situations, they consult one another, these days on the internet, and if anyone has seen the moon, the rest assume that they, too, have seen it. Hunger and husband are spelt differently.

How do the husbands reciprocate their wives' great concern for their long life? They don't have any such thing as *karvachauth* for men. And despite all the advances women have made in so many walks of life, husbands remain husbands, roof and crown of things. They realise the importance of their wives only when the ladies choose to go ahead of them in their journey to the ultimate.

During the last one year, four of my friends from old days have lost their wives, one after the other. It so happens that the sons of all of them are settled in the US. Back home in Delhi, they are left on their own. “How do you manage?” I asked Amarnath. “The part-time maid,” said he, “comes once in a day and cooks food for both times and deposits it in the fridge. I eat it as it is. I take it cold. I have become used to it.”

“Why don’t you go to the US and live with your son?” I asked him. “I can’t,” said he, “the last time I was there, his American wife wanted to push me off to a home for the aged.”

Two of the other four friends have something similar to tell. East or West, home is the best. They believe in that dictum. But they also realise in their heart of hearts that without their wives, home is not home. The poignancy of this shattered me one day last month when I learnt about Shunna, my classmate in Peshawar. I had attended his wife’s funeral. And he had told me at that time that he was going with his son to America but only for a few weeks. He was to come back quickly.

“This telephone is no longer in existence.” That was the recorded response that I got from his telephone week after week. Then one day, his brother-in-law rang me up for something. “Hasn’t Shunna returned from the States?” I asked him. “Don’t you know?” said he, “he could never go there. He died of heart attack almost immediately after my sister’s death.”

The moral of all this, to my mind, is: It is better to lose your own life than to lose your wife.

■■

At the high-level meeting of officers in the civil secretariat, a crucial question was under consideration. The usual Republic Day advertisement proclaiming that the State was marching ahead under the dynamic leadership of the Chief Minister was to be issued to the country's major newspapers. The question was: what should be the positioning of the photographs of the Prime Minister and the Chief Minister?

The layout that had been prepared by the artist showed the PM on the top left and the CM on the bottom right. Somebody had said that this could be dangerous. The opposition, already up in arms, might say that the PM was a Leftist.

From the ruling party itself someone might carry colourful tales to him. On the same analogy, an officer close to the CM had suggested that on the bottom right the CM could be labelled as a Rightist. This he might resent. He had all along wanted it to be known that he had been following the PM's middle-of-the-road policy strictly.

Past precedents were called for. It was discovered that the same pattern had been adopted for years. PM on the top left, CM on the bottom right and the State marches ahead in between – that had been the established practice and no fingers had been raised against it.

The officer close to the CM pointed out that the situation in the past was altogether different. The CM had not to air-dash to New Delhi everytime something happened in some other State. He had excellent relations with the PM. He was in his good books. But no one could say what might happen tomorrow. It was advisable to play safe. Past precedents need not be followed. The PM had himself said repeatedly that there was nothing sacrosanct about them. In such delicate matters, in any case, discretion was the better part of valour.

One of the wise old men mooted the suggestion that the advertisement might show the national emblem on the top left and the PM and the CM smiling together on the top right, with the State marching ahead below them in the rest of the space. The suggestion was rejected summarily since it was agreed that to equate the PM and the CM would be more dangerous than to put the Leftist label on the one and Rightist on the other.

The artist was called in. He came out with a simple solution – PM in the middle on the top and CM in the middle on the bottom and the State marches ahead in between. He made it clear, however, that this kind of treatment would be more pleasing to the eye in a full-page ad, and not in a half-page one, as had been envisaged. Half page would create visual confusion.

"Make it full page," whispered everybody. The finance man's objection on grounds of higher cost, particularly in the year of the drought, was over-ruled in higher interest.

The artist produced a fresh design. And the ad that emerged finally showed both the PM and the CM in the middle, one on top and the other at the bottom, vertically placed, smiling, with the State marching ahead between the two, pleasing to the eye, sans any visual confusion.

■■

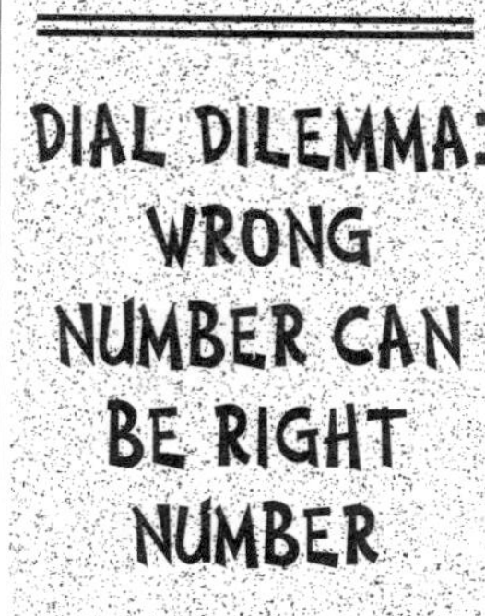

The girl from New York was pestering me. She was dialling a number but getting mine again and again. For three days the drama continued, politely, gently, like two decent people talking to each other. Then the tone of the girl's voice changed. It turned harsh. "Look," said she, "I can't figure it out. For three days I have been trying to get my father on the line. Instead, I am getting you. Something seems to be awfully wrong with the Indian telephone system, I guess."

I agreed. I had reason to agree, for the black instrument installed at my residence is either a drug addict or a yogi. Not the kind of yogi who believes in action but one who believes in meditation alone. It cares two hoots for the bell which friends say goes on ringing inside its belly and which they can hear but I can't. Not that their own instruments behave any better. Here, all telephones are alike. Some are perpetually on a fast-unto-death, some have their nerves affected (cables down) and some are victims of blackmail (*peechhe se kharabi hai*).

In any case, from pillar to post I have run umpteen times to keep alive the lovely little thing at my residence for which I pay through my nose. There is a chap called the chief general manager who sits in a strange building called Khursheed Lal Bhavan on Janpath. I managed to reach him as well.

That happened two years ago when I wrote a song in a newspaper in praise of the lovely little thing. Nothing works like flattery. The telephone started behaving like a politician asking for votes before an election. But then the election was soon over and the linesman was back. He said to me, "The manager has become chief general manager, the area manager has become general manager. *Ham to linesman ke linesman hee rahe, kaam to hameen ko karna hai* (I remain a linesman and your work has to be done by me alone)."

Back to New York. The girl over there managed to put life back into my telephone. "How is it," she asked, "that while I am dialling my father's number, which is 6439753, I am getting yours, while you say yours is 6439450." For a change," I said to the girl, "try my number which is 6439450." Miracles do happen. Half-an-hour later, my friend, D.N. Saraf, called up to say, "I am speaking from your number, 6439450, to my number, 6439753, and I thank you from the bottom of my heart for getting my daughter across to me. But tell me how this has happened?"

Before I could say anything, a voice buzzed, "6439753?" "Yes," both of us responded promptly. "Disconnect," the voice said, "for an incoming call from Bombay".

■■

Milni is one of the most beautiful parts of marriages in Northern India, particularly in Punjab. It takes place just a little before jaimala (exchange of garlands between the bride and the bridegroom) and marks the beginning of a new relationship between families, a relationship that is cemented as time goes on and makes its own contribution to the growth of the society in which we all live.

As the barat reaches the bride's place, the bridegroom riding a horse or a mare – his father, mother, grandfathers, grandmothers, sisters, brothers, countless aunts and uncles and friends dancing the bhangra ahead of him, in gay abundance, to the accompaniment of loud music from masterji's glorious band, it is received by the bride's party, equally strong, at the entrance of the pandal or hall where the rest of the ceremonies, including the all-important dinner, have to be gone through.

In bhangra, there is no such thing as enough is enough. But just as there is a time for love and a time for war, the time comes when the bridegroom's father comes forward to control the situation, after controlling himself.

The purohit takes over. He starts reciting mantras which nobody bothers to understand but which put a stop to everything else, except non-stop chirping by women. The purohit then calls upon the boy's and the girl's fathers to come forward for milni.

They put garlands around each other's necks and embrace like ardent lovers; facing the cameras which click dutifully. The girl's father then takes out from his pocket a beautiful envelope containing the milni money and slips it into the pocket of the boy's father. Simultaneously, he takes out another crisp note, circulates it around the boy's father's head as "sirwarna" and then passes it on to the band-master The boy's father does the same to him. Then comes the turn of grandfathers, uncles and all that. They follow suit.

On the 19th of August, my granddaughter, Namita's marriage to Ritesh, son of a high government officer, took place in Shimla. Even though I am quite an experienced milni man, all concerned thought it necessary to din into my ears what I had to do while having my milni with Ritesh's grandfather. And I did it competently till the moment for sirwarna came. My daughter Renu, Namita's mother, had made it quite clear to me that while the milni envelope was in the upper pocket of my coat, the sirwarna currency note was in the pocket just below.

I had never before seen Ritesh's grandfather. But the two of us got locked up so terribly that while Ritesh's grandfather did my sirwarna, I failed to do his sirwarna. I searched for the sirwarna currency note in the coat-pocket intended for it, but it was not there. I delved into every nook and corner of the pocket, scratched it, almost tearing its inside linen. The note was just not there. Still locked, and feeling somewhat uneasy, Ritesh's grandfather asked me, "Bhai sahib, what are you doing?"

"Searching the sirwarna note," I blurted out truthfully. "But why in my coat-pocket?' asked the gentleman. It was only then that I realised that my hand had let me down badly and instead of my pocket, it had slipped into Ritesh's grandfather's pocket. Of course, it made amends quickly. But I shall never forget the immense embarrassment the darned thing imposed on me.

■■

"Your Martial Majesty," said the Chief of the Intelligence Agency (CIA), "we can't bring the Taj here."

"Why?" asked Martial Majesty (MM).

"The people of Agra," said CIA, "will not be willing to part with their most precious possession. They held a big meeting in the big hall of the Subhan Allah Restaurant and decided that they would fight for the Taj to the last and our intelligence says that all of them were Muslims."

"If not the Taj," said MM, "why not the Jama Masjid of Delhi? That is where my grandfather used to pray."

"Not possible, MM," said CIA, "your grandfather's cousins and sons and nephews continue to pray there. And they will never, never allow anyone to desecrate the place of their worship."

"O.K.," said MM "bring the Red Fort. From its ramparts, I want to fly our national flag on our next national day."

"Not possible, that too, MM," said CIA, "the Red Fort is highly fortified, made of steel. It is easier to move a mountain than the Red Fort."

"Can you bring the Imambara of Lucknow to Islamabad?" asked MM, "that is what Asaf-ud-Daula got built for his deprived riyaya. The riyaya having shifted to Pakistan, the Imambara must also shift here."

"Out of the question, MM," murmured CIA, "intelligence tells us that in the process of shifting, Imambara may collapse completely. It may remain neither here nor there and even if your dream of conquering Lucknow materialises, we may not be able to see the Imambara there."

"I see," said MM, "forget about the Imambara. What about the dargah of Moin-ud-Din Chishty? It is there where Humayun prayed for a son and got Akbar from Allah." "But," submitted CIA, "the people of Ajmer will not allow us to do that. Our agency tells us that the only way we can shift the dargah from there is through prayer. But the agency also tells us that if we pray, the people of Ajmer can indulge in counter-prayer. And they are larger in number."

"How?" asked MM.

"They have," submitted CIA, "All the Muslims of India to back them. And the Muslims of India outnumber the Muslims of Pakistan,"

"What about Nizam-ud-Din Aulia's dargah in Delhi?" asked MM.

"The same holds good," said CIA, "for Nizam-ud-Din Aulia's dargah, too. There we may have to encounter greater difficulties."

"Why?"

"The Muslims of Delhi outnumber the Muslims of most towns in Pakistan. And all our towns may not fight for a mere dargah. It will take a long, long time to make them aware of its importance to Islam."

"Can't we ask," said MM, "the Muslims of India to cooperate with us in this matter? After all, they are our co-religionists."

"True," submitted CIA, "but Muslims of India are Muslims of India and not Muslims of Pakistan. Just as Muslims of Iran are Muslims of Iran and not Muslims of Pakistan.

"What do we do in the circumstances?" asked MM.

"I can't say for certain," submitted CIA, "but in my humble opinion, the best thing for us in the circumstances will be to go on nibbling at Kashmir."

■■

There was a famous minister in the Government of India who was terribly fond of culture. His clothes were cultured. His demeanour was cultured. The scent he used was cultured. The company he kept was cultured.

Once, after a hectic tour of foreign lands, along with several other members of his illustrious tribe from all over India, duly assisted by the people's most obedient servants called bureaucrats, he decided to have a bit of rest and relaxation at Kausani in Almora district of Uttaranchal from where you can get a glorious view of the magnificent Nandadevi range in the Himalayas early in the morning.

It must be said that the hon'ble minister deserved his holiday. He had roamed about all over the USA and Europe, along with his gang, closely studying how the roads over there were kept neat and clean. I was deputed to cover his sojourn in Kausani. The minister was staying in the Circuit House. I was in the Forest Rest House. Next to me in the same rest house was the Sub-Divisional Magistrate of the area. His duty was to maintain law and order, whatever that meant, around the minister's abode.

The minister stayed there for nearly a week. During that period, the SDM and I became a bit close to each other. One night, after dinner, I heard a lot of boisterous noise coming from the side of the district board rest house down below. A big black Buick car had steamed in. I thought something potentially dangerous had occurred and knocked at the door of the SDM's room. He came out and, rubbing his eyes, looked at the Buick and pulled me into his room.

His orderly prepared coffee for the two of us. As we were sipping it and as I asked him questions about the Buick and its passengers to satisfy my curiosity, the SDM said philosophically, "You know, there is nothing unusual about his tamasha. The Buick belongs to the overseer sahib. He comes here off and on along with his contractors and they have a gala night".

Overseer sahib! A minor clog in the government's machine! How could he afford to keep a Buick? The SDM enlightened me, "he is the brother of the wife of the Chief Minister's grandson and nobody can touch him. Construction of roads in the hills is 10 times costlier than in the planes. He constructs, through his contractors, roads on the plateau down below and shows them as having been constructed on the mountains. Besides, he gets a hefty commission from every contractor who works for him".

"Why don't you catch him?" being a bloody fool, I put that question to the SDM. "And lose my job?" he said instantaneously. "There are certain things over which you have to have your eyes closed. So many before me have come and gone. None has been able to touch him."

I could not help recalling that incident as holidaying at my daughter Renu's place in Shimla, I read all the colourful stories that have been appearing in the Press about a fellow carted Ravi Sidhu, ex-chairman of the Punjab PSC, and the gentlemen on whom he had been daring enough to inflict unmerited greatness. That he came from my fraternity, journalism, is a matter of shame to me. But what were the masters he served doing? Why did everybody keep his eyes closed?

Perhaps another foreign jaunt by ministers and bureaucrats is called for this time, to discover how to prevent others from noticing what you wish them not to notice.

■■

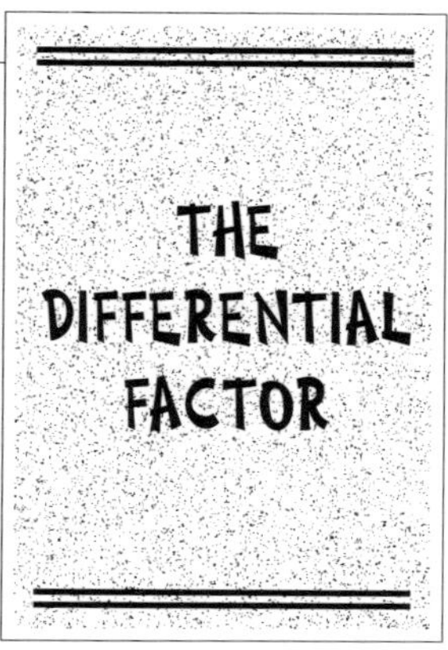

THE DIFFERENTIAL FACTOR

I do not know where the Durand Line is, but at Turkham, Pakistan's border with Afghanistan, there is a long, broad white line running down the Hindukush mountains dividing them, so it appears, into two parts. On one side lies Pakistan, on the other an uphill road takes you on to Afghanistan. There is an iron gate with miles of barbed wire fencing running on either side intended to prevent people from crossing the border.

That fencing and that white line, drawn by man or nature, were also visible from a distance when I visited Turkham the last time – in 1946. The fencing could not check the to-and-fro movement of people living on the Khyber Pass and the rugged mountains around. There was hardly any difference between the tribals living on either side of the borderline. They all looked alike.

"Keep your hand on your pistol," said Shirin Dil Khan to me, as we walked to the first cave on the Hindukush on this side of the border. Shirin was a Captain in the Indian Army deputed to receive some Afghan cadets who had been selected for training in the Indian military academy in Dehra Dun. He had picked me up from the Islamic College, Peshawar, where I was doing my post-graduation. That was against regulations but we were old buddies and Shirin had taken the risk.

He had his service revolver with him. I had my licensed pistol. Time was aplenty, so we got an opportunity to have a peep into the life of the tribals. They were living in caves and huts far away from the reach of what is called civilisation. No outsider was allowed to get close to them. They were always at war with one another – clannish wars inherited from generation to generation, fought mostly on three issues: money, women and land.

The moment we reached the first hut, it became obvious to us that we were not welcome. Half a dozen middle-aged men, unkept and uncouth, with ferocity writ large on their battered faces, surrounded us menacingly and subjected us to a shower of awkward questions which had but one meaning, "How dare you walk into our territory?"

"Let's get out of here before anything happens," said Shirin. "They can kill us for our arms." Hurriedly, we retreated from the place. All along my heart thumped loud in fear of being sliced in the throat by some angry tribal.

Arms were dear to those fellows. They used to manufacture them in underground factories and smuggle them to Peshawar, Bannu, Kohat and other neighbouring places. To augment earnings from that, they used to invade those very neighbouring places and loot the people living there. The British treated the entire tribal area as a battlefield intended to keep their troops in operational fitness. At the same time, they refrained from interfering in the internal affairs of the tribals.

Have things changed in those parts? Yes and no. Crude arms have yielded place to AK-47s. For smuggling of hashish, the area has enlarged, extending up to New York. And for loot and plunder, apart from the neighbouring towns, there are places as far away as Kashmir and Karachi. But no outsider is still allowed to intrude into the tribal hamlets.

The other day, newspaper reports tell us, two Pakistani Captains in uniform strayed into one of those hamlets by mistake. They were taken prisoners at once and the Pakistani Army had to use armoured vehicles to rescue their life.

Slumbering somewhere deep down within me, my old buddy, Shirin, raises his head. I find him rubbing his eyes and whispering to me. "Fifty years ago, but for the grace of God, instead of those two fellows, it might have been you and I."

■■

NO RETURN TICKET AVAILABLE FROM HERE

I recently ran into a small, exhilirating display of posters done by little kids along the outer wall of their school in the Alaknanda area of New Delhi. "We would like to share with you," proclaimed the display in bold letters, "what we have learnt in our school."

One of the posters which drew my attention in particular carried the sketch of an aeroplane belonging to Air Nicotine. The caption atop it said: "Fly Now and Pay Later." I jotted down the message that followed. It said: "We can fly you to many destinations. These include lung cancer, paralytic attack, mouth cancer, food pipe cancer, bladder cancer, still birth, impotence, bronchitis, emphysema. Most of them lead to the Great Getaway – a heart stopping experience that snatches your breath away. Four million of our best customers will reach there.....

"Free gifts for all customers. On boarding, every customer will get bad breath, stained teeth, smelly clothes, cough..... Special youth offer. We catch you young. If you start as a teenager, you will be our privileged customer and the chances of your early trip to the Great Getaway are very high.....

Frequent flyers awards – the more you use Air Nicotine, the sooner you will reach the destination through special bookings and superfast carriers. Free tickets for your family......

Down below, on the left side of the poster several carriers for surface transport were mentioned. These included cigarettes, bidi, cigar, pipe, hookah, chillum, gutka, snuff and zarda.

Apparently, some teacher had guided the students in doing that display. The print line mentioned the name of a professor from the All-India Institute of Medical Sciences. As I jotted down the contents of the poster, my mind went back to early nineties when

I had my first massive heart attack. "Do you smoke," the good Dr Lochan in the Batra Hospital, where I was taken, had asked me while examining my X-ray. "I used to smoke pipe," I replied guiltily "but I gave it up years ago." That was too late. He did not say that. But it was apparent to me.

Six years later, when I had to go through heart bypass surgery in the same hospital, Dr Upinder Kaul, head of the cardiology department there, put to me the same question. And I gave him the same answer.

I am fairly all right now, though I have to take all the precautions and drugs regularly. We can't change our yesterdays into todays but as I scribble these lines, after seeing that display by the kids, I am reminded of a long short story by the great Russian Nobel laureate, for literature Alexander Solzhenistyn. In that story, the hero is exiled to a remote inhospitable place in the erstwhile USSR for raising his voice against Stalin and all that he stood for. One of the things that he sees on the platform of the railway station of the city to which he is exiled is a billboard which proclaims loudly. No Return Tickets Available From Here.

■■

The more I think of Pakistan's CEO, Pervez Musharraf, the more I am reminded of Khan Aflatoon of Jhang Maghiana. Who was Khan Aflatoon? Not many of the present generation would know that. But old-timers may recall that among the Hotianas, Khotianas, Tiwanas and Diwanas of Sir Sikander Hayat Khan's Cabinet in good old undivided Punjab in good old undivided India, he was the one who stood head and shoulders above the rest.

May his soul rest in peace! I recall one day his PA's mother-in-law died. The PA had to rush to his village. He could not contact Khan Aflatoon. He just left the telegram he had received from home on the table of Khan Aflatoon and took the first train to wherever he was to go. When Khan Aflatoon returned to office from a Cabinet meeting or something like that and saw the telegram on his table, he started weeping zar-zar (profusely). It was much later that he made two great discoveries. One, the telegram was not intended for him. Two, his mother-in-law had kicked the bucket long, long before his PA's had thought it fit to do that.

Khan Aflatoon was in love with things old, including old socks. They say that he changed his socks only when the socks developed more holes than these could possibly be put up with. Old socks, like stale fish, throw up awful smell. Khan Aflatoon's dutiful wife always made sure that he did change his socks before going to the Chief Minister's residence. She managed to exercise an effective check on this. But then one evening, as she was going along with Khan Aflatoon, to Sir Sikander Hayat Khan's place for dinner, she found the smell oozing out of Khan Aflatoon's well-polished shoes rather too powerful.

"Haven't you changed your socks?" she asked Khan Aflatoon.

"I knew," said he, "that you would put to me this question. For your general knowledge, I beg to say that I did change my socks. And as proof thereof, I have brought in my pocket, to show to you, the old pair as well."

Khan Aflatoon and his wife were going on a boat cruise on the Ravi. In mid-stream, the boatman said that his boat was getting flooded and there was the danger that all three of them, Khan Aflatoon, his wife and the boatman, were going to be sunk."

"Why?" asked Khan Aflatoon.

"The boat," said the boatman, "has developed a small hole and water has started coming on to the boat through it. The hole is getting bigger and bigger and the danger is that by that time I can take the boat back to the river-bank, the boat will be flooded and once it is flooded, all three of us will be drowned."

"Oh jhalia (simpleton)," said Khan Aflatoon to the boatman, "where is your akkal (intelligence) gone? Such a small thing and you are shivering as if you have developed high fever. Why don't you dig another hole in the boat and allow the water that comes in through the hole you are talking about to get out of the one I am suggesting to you?"

God knows what happened thereafter. But as I think of Pervez Musharraf, and I think of him every day because of his great expertise in hijacking petty things like democracy, justice, liberty and all that, I am reminded of Khan Aflatoon who must have become dear to the Lord long before Musharraf was born.

■■

Three days earlier, Netaji had requested me to meet him on Sunday. That, he said, was the only day on which he could relax a bit. Even though he had ceased to be a minister some years back, the demand on his time had always been very heavy.

There were numerous causes, from spiritual awakening to family planning, to which Netaji was passionately devoted. These kept him almost constantly on the move, more often abroad than in India. I once asked him where all the funds came from. He shrugged his shoulders and said, God takes care of those who take care of others.

On the appointed day, Netaji sent his air-conditioned Maruti 1000 car to my place and a little later I was closeted with him in the drawing room of his sprawling bungalow in a posh locality in South Delhi. "We have," Netaji informed me, "floated a new organisation – Peace through Fight against Fundamentalism. PFF is its abbreviation. We are holding its first national conference in New Delhi next month and that is why I have bothered you."

Netaji gave me the names of some illustrious people, in power and out of power, who had agreed to be associated with the new organisation and then asked me how I was placed. "I mean," he added, "I want you to write the presidential address of the chairman of the conference and also my own key-note address.

"The chairman will dwell on fundamentalism. I'd like to restrict myself to terrorism. I may touch on fundamentalism also, but there is no point in repeating what the presidential address says.

"I can write the speeches myself. But, as you know, I don't get time even to scratch my head. For old times' sake, please don't say 'no' to me. The services of my stenographer are at your disposal. I shall personally take care of all your other needs."

Having done a good deal of ghost-writing for some of the country's prominent leaders in the days gone by, I was not prepared to get back into the rut again. And so I tried to wriggle out of the situation by stating that I had not done any study of fundamentalism or terrorism and hence might not be able to do justice to the two subjects.

Netaji was, however, quite insistent. He had mentioned the great difficulties he had to grapple with at the cost of his own health in setting up the PFF. "The twin evils of fundamentalism and terrorism," he asserted, "are eating into the vitals of our country. We are launching a crusade against them. l do expect you to let us have the benefit of your assistance."

Netaji comes from one of the northern states which are currently in the grip of terrorism. I wanted to ask him to go to his state and to fight against the twin evils along with the people living there. I did not say so but I did manage to gather the courage to suggest that it would be better to hold the conference there.

"And be kidnapped or shot dead?" was his spontaneous retort. Netaji realised quickly that this retort was somewhat indiscreet. He felt embarrassed and almost ran short of words. But then, shrewd as he was, he recovered quickly and explained to me that all the leaders associated with him were hard-pressed for time. "Most of them," he said, "are based in Delhi. To make arrangements elsewhere, and to take them there will be difficult. It will cause further strain on the already over-stretched resources of the security agencies."

"That will be unpatriotic. Besides, they will need several months' notice. And to us, time is crucial. Every day that passes claims more lives. We cannot postpone the conference. We have already fixed the dates and these just cannot be changed." Netaji also underscored the point that holding the conference in Delhi would have an added advantage. "Here," he elaborated, "it will catch the attention of the national and the international media."

"The battle of Waterloo was won on the playgrounds of Eton. Why can't the battle against fundamentalism and terrorism in Punjab, Jammu & Kashmir, and elsewhere in India be won from the conference halls of Delhi?"

I was amused by Netaji's convoluted logic. He ordered more tea for me.

As his man brought it, a telephone call came from Tokyo. According to it, there was to be a conference on Buddhism somewhere in Japan. It was to be followed by a four-week tour of places of Buddhist importance in various parts of the world. The caller invited Netaji to attend the conference and join the tour. He said he had already despatched two return tickets – one for Netaji and the other for his spouse. "I am sorry," Netaji said to me, "in the newly-created circumstances, we will have to postpone our conference on fundamentalism to some other time. I will get in touch with you on my return from abroad."

■■

"What is this case?" asked the minister, visibly annoyed. "You have passed it on to me without even seeing it."

"I have seen it, Sir," said the secretary. "The case has been explained at length by the joint secretary in his note, and the additional secretary has summed it up for your convenience."

"But you have not given your own views on it," grumbled the minister. "You have just passed it on to me for orders. As if I have nothing else to do...."

"If you permit, Sir," submitted the secretary, "the joint secretary will explain it to you. He has gone deep into the matter."

The minister looked at the joint secretary disdainfully. The latter looked at his boss wistfully. "Very well," said the minister, passing on the file to the joint secretary, "let us hear what he has to say."

The joint secretary opened the file, coughed without any ostensible provocation, cleared his throat, and then, burying his head into the file, blurted out, "Sir, on pages 41 to 45, the hill area development scheme has been explained in a nutshell. It was part of the seventh five-year plan. Under this scheme, all the villages in the hills were to be connected by *pucca* roads.

"Now, Sir, the cost of constructing a road that runs through mountains, I mean, where the cutting of huge rocks and boulders is involved, is 10 to 20 times higher than the cost of building roads in the plains. In this case, most of the roads were constructed in the plateaus. The cost there is almost the same as in the plains."

"Pages 50 to 54 give the details of the roads that were supposed to have been constructed. The subsequent three pages give details of such of these roads as were supposed to have been repaired within less than three months. On page 55 are the names of the villages that were connected by these roads."

The joint secretary paused here, not for breath but in the hope that from that point on the secretary would take over. The latter refused to oblige.

"The roads were constructed?" queried the minister, fiddling with the diamond and ruby rings on his finger.

"Yes, Sir," answered the joint secretary.

"Then what is your complaint?" demanded the minister.

"Sir," said the joint secretary, "I have no complaint. But two things have come out. One, while the roads were constructed in the plateaus, the expenditure incurred on them was calculated on the basis of hill roads. And two, 50 per cent of the villages connected by these roads do not exist."

"Have you visited them?" asked the minister angrily.

"No, Sir," replied the secretary.

"But aren't you expected to be the watch-dog of democracy, assisting me in such maters?" shouted the minister.

"Yes, Sir," submitted the joint secretary, "but how can I visit villages that do not exist?"

"In that case, you can go now."

Having dismissed him, the minister turned to the secretary. "What is the recommendation of your great deputy, the additional secretary?" he asked.

"He has suggested that the case should be handed over to the CBI."

"And having said that, he has conveniently proceeded on leave?"

"Yes, Sir."

"There is something fishy in this," said the minister, "I suspect that you, the joint secretary and the additional secretary are conspiring to give a bad name to my kith and kin. And also to tarnish the image of the government and the party. There may be some foreign hand behind this conspiracy."

The secretary kept quiet.

"Under whose supervision were the roads constructed?" asked the minister.

"The ultimate responsibility," explained the secretary, "rests with the chairman of the backward areas development board. I am sorry to say, Sir, that he is somewhat unmindful of his relationship with you. He visited the hill areas a number of times when the roads were under construction. Earlier, you will recall, Sir, the green valley reclamation scheme was handled by him personally."

"What was that?"

"You will remember, Sir, under that scheme more Iand was sold – of course, at concessional rates – to the backward sectors of the society than was actually reclaimed."

"Yes, yes, what happened to that case?"

"It is pending, Sir."

"Let this one, too, remain, pending."

The secretary went back to his room, called the joint secretary handed over the file to him and asked him to keep it.

"How many have you got?" asked the secretary.

"Scores of them," said the joint secretary. "Some of them I have inherited from my predecessor, some he had inherited from his predecessor and the rest have come up during my own tenure. I have shown the entire list to you. Some of the files pertain to the sixth five-year plan period. Two almirahs in my room are full of pending cases. This is a dangerous situation. "Never mind," philosophised the secretary, "We are passing through dangerous times. Remember, one of the basic principles of the administration in our country is that public memory is short. You take care of your predecessors. Your successors will take care of you. That is how the system goes on. Let us not become its martyrs."

■■

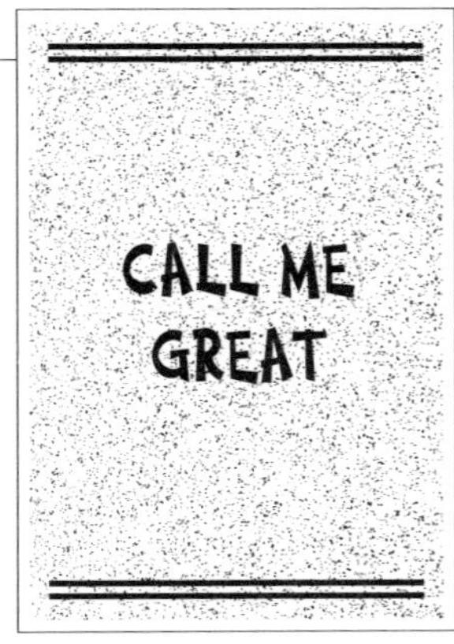

"See here," said the minister, "I want to appear as I am."

"Yes, Sir," said the secretary. "That is the instruction I have given to the information officer and he has spoken to those TV fellows. He has given them a detailed brief on your rich past."

"How is it then," asked the minister, "that I am seldom shown on television? There are others," he gave the names of some of his colleagues, "who are seen in almost every bulletin. Sometimes they are addressing party workers, sometimes women, sometimes children, sometimes just nobody."

"Sir," submitted the secretary, blushing, "you don't need any artificial aids to click with the people. You are already a big hit with them. Of course, you are entitled to more coverage. I will myself speak to the top person in Doordarshan."

The minister rubbed his chin, took out a folded betel-leaf from a small ornamental silver box lying on his table, pushed it into his open mouth, rubbed his chin again and said, "Have you told them of the *andolans* (movements) I have launched and led?"

"Yes, Sir," asserted the secretary, "I have personally vetted the brief that was prepared by your office. It lays particular stress on your great role in the trade union movement in your state; how, after your expulsion from school..."

"I was not expelled," the minister interrupted him angrily, "I just dropped out."

"Yes, Sir," said the secretary.

"You just dropped out. And then by dint of your own hard work, you became the president of the managing committee of the same school and later established a number of other schools as well as your great education trust. That apart, the brief highlights the fact that you were the first to set up a rickshaw-pullers' association in the country and that this association organised big demonstrations all over the state to welcome the hike in the price of petrol in the wake of the Gulf war. 'Back to the wheel' was its motto and the inspiration for this motto came to you from Gandhiji's spinning wheel.

"There are three. comprehensive paragraphs in the brief on your 'Back to the wheel' movement. There is also a detailed description of your heroic role in the freedom struggle..."

"Freedom struggle?" grinned the minister.

"Sir," chuckled the secretary, "I mean freedom from want, hunger and poverty. Unfortunately, you were not born when the struggle against the British was going on, but then you are a born fighter and this fact has been taken care of in the brief.

"I shall personally tell the Doordarshan people that if you are holding this important portfolio, it is no favour to you. It is because of your glorious deep-rooted past and equally glorious potential for the future of the country."

As the secretary looked at the minister for approval, the latter said, "I appreciate what you are doing. And to tell you the truth, I am not bothered about TV. But they should strike a proper balance. That is what autonomy of the media means.

"I have an idea. Why not call the rickshaw union to my residence? They will be happy to come and felicitate me."

"You mean rickshaw-*wallas* from your constituency?" queried the secretary.

"Of course, from my constituency," said the minister. "Get in touch with Tarzon."

"Great idea, Sir," said the secretary. "We can always pay them, I mean the cost of journey etc. out of your discretionary grant. I shall fix the date in consultation with Tarzon*ji* and inform those TV fellows in time."

The date was fixed. Those TV fellows were duly cautioned. But by the time the rickshaw-*wallas* were brought to the residence of the minister, day had turned into night and the darkness that followed had swallowed the gentleman. The government had fallen.

The rickshaw-*wallas* had been wise enough to claim and get their money in advance. Tarzon*ji* vanished from the scene.

■■

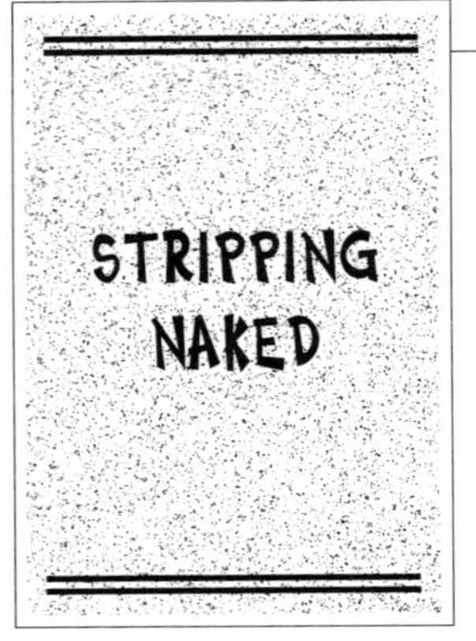

How long does winter last in Delhi? Just about three months – November, December and January. This brief period upsets our domestic budget more than any other quarter of the year.

It demands that we have good quilts and blankets to protect ourselves against the biting cold. How many of us can afford to buy new quilts and blankets every other year? Not many. Most of us live on a shoe-string sort of budget. We resurrect the old *razais* (quilts), bought long ago, do a bit of patchwork, and manage life with them till winter ends its sport with us.

But so far as woollen clothes and jerseys are concerned, it is an altogether different thing. Our kids and grand-kids need new ones every year. Their physical dimensions keep growing. And whether you like it or not, they are active participants in the phenomenon of changing modes and moods. They won't like to be left behind by it.

Personally, I like winter. Coming as I do from Peshawar, where winter used to be long and severe, I love everything that it brings along with it – from invigorating walks in the early hours of the morning to reading and writing till late in the night. Earlier, about a decade or so ago, when I was in the service of our benign Government, in winter months I used to avoid going on tour to places like Madras (now Chennai) and Bombay (now Mumbai) which do not have any winter.

"Oh wind, if winter comes, can spring be far behind?" Shelley was right. But that was in relation to England. If he had lived in Delhi, he might have said, "Oh wind, if summer comes, can winter be far behind?"

What pinches me most during winter in Delhi is the dry-cleaner. Last year, he charged Rs 20 per suit. This year it has gone up to Rs 25. Money apart, I do not know what kind of dry-cleaning he does. Every time I send him a suit, it comes back home lighter. His explanation: "It sheds off the dust it accumulates during the previous winter."

By that standard, as a nation we should be lighter in weight. A casual look at our politicians would suggest that that is not the case. Maybe they do not shed off the dust they accumulate. And maybe they accumulate more of it than the rest of us.

Fortunately I do not need more woollen suits than I have. Temptations do come my way. And though I have a young heart, I manage to resist them. But what could I do when my son, Prem, brought for me a suit-length from abroad in selecting which, as he said, he had to invest almost half a day?

"Why don't you get a suit made for yourself?" I asked him. "No," he asserted vehemently, "this is for you and you alone. It will go very well with you."

To underscore his point, he took me to a draper's shop in Greater Kailash-I, where I was surveyed, assessed and measured duly and asked to come next week for the thing called trial. "How much would be the charge?" I enquired from the bulky gentleman with the long tape hanging round his neck like a doctor's stethoscope.

"Fifteen hundred rupees, for you only, Sir," he said in the manner of one doing me a great favour.

I felt like leaving the cloth behind and running away from the place.

On the way back home, my son mumbled something about the shop being the best in South Delhi. Good old Josh Malihabadi came to my mind. Jawaharlal Nehru was one of the great patrons of the great poet. He used to invite him to the Teen Murti House off and on.

One evening he asked him for his latest. Josh asked for a glass of whisky. Nehru arranged it for him. And then Josh gave him the latest.

It was on bribery.

The first line said, "If we do not take bribe, what shall we eat?" The last but one said, "*woh silahi li mian darzi nehn, ke nanga kar diya* (the tailor charged so much, that I was stripped naked)."

■■

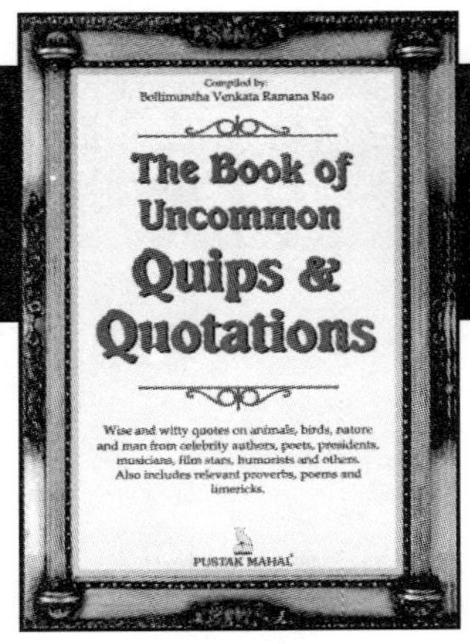

The Book of Uncommon Quips & Quotations

—Bollimuntha Venkata Ramana Rao

Life is always the greatest teacher. But reading about the experiences and words of others is also a great form of learning. The wise and witty quotes in this book can teach one more in a few hours' reading than a lifetime of bumbling around. Many of the quotes are uncommon and will not have been read before by most readers.

The Book of Uncommon Quips & Quotations also includes meaningful proverbs, poems and limericks. The focus of this book, though, is more on animals, nature and man. Many quotes stress the importance of compassion towards all our fellow creatures that inhabit the earth. The quotations include those of celebrity authors, poets, presidents, musicians, film stars, humorists and others.

Demy Size • Pages: 128
Price: Rs. 80/- • Postage: Rs. 15/-

2000 Titbits & Satires

—*M.S. Choubey*

Look Deep into Immumerable Facts of Your Behaviour!

The author of this book has always remained a keen student of art and literature — although a petroleum geologist by profession. He goes deep into the mode of human activities in different styles in day-to-day life through his inquisitive mind.

This book presents a treasure of 2000 humorous titbits and satires on 351 varied shades on every spehere of human life.

Outlook-changing 2000 Ifs expose, in their unique way, the subtleties of human nature, its varied characteristics by touching 351 topics. Arranged in alphabetical order, the author has offered his comments on different modes of human activities all in a way that make them very witty, humorous and satirical, having all its sentences starting with the same word 'If'.

☞ If one takes life seriously, the book has enough serious satires to offer.

☞ If one takes life as it comes—the book has enough material with which to laugh it off.

☞ If the book is found to be a sad commentary on our frail little existence, everyone will take to read it again in that light!

The book is the only one of its type in the world having all its sentences starting with the same world 'If'.

Demy Size • Pages: 176
Price: Rs. 68/- • Postage: Rs. 15/-

Amusing Encounters of Daily Life

—Tanushree Podder

True tales that will make you grin & guffaw

The most precious moments of life are those that bring a smile to our face. We recollect only the moments, which bring us extreme joy or extreme unhappiness. While the happy times glide away with an amazing speed, it is the tragic times that seem to linger forever. The slippery moments of joy slip so easily out of our hands, leaving us craving for more.

Ideally, we should just remember the moments of enjoyment and laughter at the end of the day. What could be a better way to end the day than to read something light and bubbly? This anthology of humorous writings is designed to help you unwind. Just the medicine your doctor would prescribe!

Demy Size • Pages: 128
Price: Rs. 68/- • Postage: Rs. 15/-